SO-EIG-076

Jesus
SEND YOUR SPIRIT

A Confirmation Catechesis
for Junior High School

Janie Gustafson, Ph.D.
Rev. Gerard P. Weber, S.T.L.

BENZIGER PUBLISHING COMPANY
Mission Hills, California

Special Editorial Consultant:
Irene H. Murphy

Contributing Editor:
Michael Amodei

Cover Photography:
Stephen McBrady

Photography:
Stephen McBrady (5, 8, 9, 10, 19, 22, 23, 26, 27, 33, 36, 37, 38, 39, 41, 42, 43, 47, 50, 51, 53, 55, 56, 61, 64, 65, 66, 68/r, 70, 75, 78, 79, 80, 82, 84, 89, 92, 94, 101, 103, 106, 108, 109, 110, 111)
Megan McKenna (52, 96)
Bob Messina (67)
Paul A. Pavlick (12/r, 107)
Photo Edit: Myrleen Ferguson (12/l, 28, 83); Titian, *Christ Holding the Orb*, Leningrad, The Hermitage (95)
Jerome Riordan (24, 68/l)
Stacie Smith-Rowe (11, 93, 97)
Special thanks to the Most Reverend Juan A. Arzube, Vicar General of the San Gabriel Region, Archdiocese of Los Angeles, for his cooperation with photography.

Illustrations:
Kevin Davidson (13, 14, 25, 40, 54, 69, 81, 98, 112)
Christa Kieffer (59, 60, 90, 91, 101, 102)
Jim McConnell (62, 73, 74, 104, 115, 116)
Norman Merritt (48, 49)
Barbara Rhodes (20, 21, 31, 32)
Cyndie Salans Rosenheim (34, 35, 45, 46, 77, 87, 88)
Joann Slater (6, 7, 17, 18)

Nihil Obstat:
Sr. Angela M. Hallahan, C.H.F.
Censor Deputatus

Imprimatur:
†Roger M. Mahony
Archbishop of Los Angeles
February 7, 1989

The nihil obstat and imprimatur are official declarations that a book or pamphlet is free of doctrinal or moral error. No implication is contained therein that those who have granted the nihil obstat and imprimatur agree with the contents, opinions, or statements expressed.

Copyright © 1990 by Glencoe Publishing Company, a division of Macmillan, Inc. All rights reserved. No part of this book may be reproduced or transmitted in any form or by any means, electronic or mechanical, including photocopying, recording, or by any information storage and retrieval system, without permission in writing from the Publisher.

Send all inquiries to:
Benzinger Publishing Company
15319 Chatsworth Street, P.O. Box 9509
Mission Hills, California 91345-9509

Printed in the United States of America
ISBN 0-02-652480-5
    5 6 7 8 9   93 92

Contents

A Letter to the Student

Therefore, I, too, hearing of your faith in the Lord Jesus and of your love for all the holy ones, do not cease giving thanks for you, remembering you in my prayers, that the God of our Lord Jesus Christ, the Father of glory, may give you a spirit of wisdom and revelation resulting in knowledge of Him. May the eyes of your hearts be enlightened, that you may know what is the hope that belongs to His call, what are the riches of glory in His inheritance among the holy ones, and what is the surpassing greatness of His power for us who believe. . . *(Ephesians 1:15–19).*

Saint Paul wrote these words to the new Christians at Ephesus, in Turkey, almost 20 centuries ago. But he might just as well have meant these words for you.

For many years now, you have been living and growing as a baptized Catholic. You have shown your faith and your love in many different ways. At this time, the Catholic community invites you to take the next step in your journey of faith. You are being invited to celebrate the sacrament of Confirmation.

This book—*Jesus, Send Your Spirit*—is meant to help you prepare for your Confirmation. The book is an invitation, too. Through stories and questions, prayers and activities, this book asks you to open yourself to the Holy Spirit—the "spirit of wisdom and revelation" that Saint Paul talks about.

This book also reminds you of the resources you have been given to help you on your journey. Among these resources are the gifts of the Holy Spirit (wisdom, knowledge, reverence, courage, understanding, right judgment, and wonder and awe) and the gift of faith that is expressed in the Apostles' Creed.

If you look at the Contents page, you will see that *Jesus, Send Your Spirit* is made up of eight chapters. Each chapter begins with a story about one of the challenges, or important questions, that you face on your journey of faith. The text then explores how a gift of the Holy Spirit can help you face this challenge, and how the gift of faith (as expressed in an article of the Creed) helps bring everything together. Each chapter also gives you opportunities to apply what you have learned to your own life, to review the content of the lesson, to prepare in some practical way for your Confirmation, and to celebrate in prayer.

At the back of this book is a Handbook section that will be useful to you throughout your preparation for Confirmation. The Handbook contains a glossary of religious terms, a collection of traditional Catholic prayers and actions, some important lists to keep in mind, and a review of the Mass and of the sacrament of Reconciliation.

We hope you enjoy preparing for Confirmation with *Jesus, Send Your Spirit*. Along with your family, your teachers, your sponsor, and your whole parish community, we join our prayer for you with Saint Paul's: May the Holy Spirit be with you as you grow in faith, hope, and love!

Created in God's Image

In This Chapter

- You will grow in your appreciation of your Catholic identity, and of the part that faith plays in developing that identity.
- You will learn about the Holy Spirit's gift of wisdom.
- You will realize that God loves and cares for you.

The Challenge

- To accept myself as God created me
- To believe that God cares about me
- To look at the importance of the sacrament of Confirmation in my life

Maria's Decision

Maria stood at her bedroom mirror, combing her hair. In the mirror, she could see her friend Shannon sitting on the floor, sorting through a pile of music tapes.

"I love coming over here," Shannon said over the blare of the music. "You have the best tapes!"

Maria frowned at her own reflection. "Hey, that's what happens when your parents get divorced," she said, trying to make a joke out of it. "You get twice as many presents."

"Not bad," Shannon sighed enviously.

"Actually," Maria replied as she continued to fuss with her hair, "it's pretty awful."

Shannon looked up. She caught Maria's eye in the mirror, and turned down the music. "OK, what's wrong?" Shannon asked, with the intuition of an old friend.

Maria put down the comb. "Oh, nothing, really. I'm just sort of . . . worried."

"Yeah," Shannon teased, "worried that Eddie won't call."

"Eddie's got nothing to do with it!" Maria flopped down on the floor next to Shannon. "If you promise not to tell. . . ."

"I swear," Shannon answered quickly.

"I got accepted at Powell High for next year."

Shannon's eyes got wide. "Wow! The science school? The school that only takes the top five percent of kids in the whole city?"

Maria nodded.

"So what's the problem? You're going to go, aren't you?"

"I don't know," Maria said quietly. "It's like I'm being pulled in a lot of different directions. Mom says Powell's a great opportunity, and it'll help with college and a career and all of that stuff. Dad says it's too far away and too expensive. If I decide to go to Powell, Dad will say I'm siding with Mom. And if I don't go, Mom'll say I listen to Dad too much."

"Got it," Shannon said, nodding. "But what do *you* want to do?"

"I want the whole thing to go away!" Maria laughed. "But no, honestly—the big problem is that I don't know *what* I want. I'm not even sure who I am today, never mind what I want to be ten years from now. All I keep thinking about are my friends. I mean, you and Tina and Eddie and Mike and me—we've been together since pre-school! How can I go off to Powell by myself?"

"So you're saying that if you go to Powell, we won't get to hang around together?"

"That's not what I *want*," Maria answered seriously, "but I'm trying to get real about this. If I'm at Powell and you're not, we'll meet new people. We'll do different stuff. I'm afraid . . . we won't be friends anymore."

Shannon grinned. "Sure," she said, "anything's possible. But if you think I'm going to lose track of you *or* your tape collection, you're nuts!" She looked at her friend. "C'mon, Maria—what's the *real* problem?"

Maria spoke very softly. "What if I mess up? What if after all that tuition money and everything, I find out I just can't cut it, or I hate science or something?"

"You? No way! You'll do great at Powell, I just know it."

"I wish I believed that," Maria answered truthfully.

"I wish you did, too." Shannon hugged Maria. "And I wish I could tell you what to do. But I'm not you."

"I know," Maria said. "And thanks. But I guess this is one decision I'm going to have to make on my own."

Think It Over/Write About It

1. Do you think Maria really knows herself very well? Why or why not?
2. What are two clues that show that Maria does not think very highly of herself?
3. Create an ending for this story. Tell what Maria's decision will be, and why.
4. If you were in Maria's situation, what would *you* do? Why?

A Sense of Identity

Do you ever think about who you are and where you are going? Have you ever wondered what you will be doing in the future? If so, you've had an experience of being human. In one way or another, all people ask themselves two basic questions: "Who am I?" and "Where do I find meaning?"

These questions deal with a sense of *identity*. Identity is a concern throughout our lives, but there are certain times when these questions seem to carry extra force and importance. The early teen years, with so many changes and choices, are one of those times.

Having a sense of identity means knowing who we are. In the story, Maria's sense of identity is not yet developed. She's not quite sure what she wants. She doesn't have a clear view of her own abilities and strengths.

In fact, Maria has low self-esteem. *Self-esteem* is the way we feel about our identity. People with high self-esteem feel "at home" with themselves. People with low self-esteem, on the other hand, often feel unsure of themselves. They find it hard to believe that they're "good enough" to be loved or to succeed in life.

Developing a strong sense of identity and high self-esteem is a very important part of growing up. This challenge is not limited to our physical or emotional identity; it's a challenge to our spiritual growth, as well.

Catholic Identity

Being Catholic is an important part of our spiritual identity. At Baptism, the Catholic Church accepted us as new members. We were invited to form a personal relationship with God. In a public ceremony, our parents, godparents, and family members responded to that invitation in our name. They promised to help form our identity, with the help of God and of the whole Church.

Our Catholic identity, like our own self-esteem, is not just something that is handed to us by others. We help to shape it when we pray and participate in the sacraments—especially the Eucharist and Reconciliation. When we study and ask questions about God and about our faith, we are actively shaping our Catholic identity.

Choosing to Grow

At this time in your life, you are being offered a special opportunity to develop your Catholic identity. You are being invited to confirm, or strengthen, your membership in the Church through the sacrament of *Confirmation*. Like Baptism and the Eucharist, Confirmation is a *sacrament of initiation*. It makes a public statement about who you are and where you belong. It celebrates your choice to continue growing as a follower of Jesus Christ.

The decision to be confirmed is a big one. It will call upon all your sense of identity and self-esteem. But this is not a decision you have to make by yourself. Your family, your friends, the person you will choose to sponsor you, and the whole Catholic community are there to support you. The Holy Spirit is with you, too—guiding you and stirring to life in you the gifts that will help you continue to grow throughout your whole life.

The Gift of Wisdom

We could all use help in making decisions—and in living up to the consequences of the decisions we make. It's that kind of help that Maria was looking for in the story. On a simple, everyday level, the kind of help we look for is what our parents call "just good common sense." Developing common sense is part of growing up, part of forming a sense of identity.

In the sacrament of Confirmation, the Holy Spirit enriches our growing common sense with the gift of *wisdom*. The word "wisdom" comes from a Greek word meaning "to see clearly." The Holy Spirit's gift of wisdom gives us a new way of looking at life. We

Religious Vocabulary

Identity The sense of who we are and what we can do.

Self-esteem The way we feel about who we are. People with high self-esteem feel good about themselves. They have a clear view of their own abilities.

Confirmation One of the seven sacraments of the Church. Confirmation celebrates the presence of the Holy Spirit in our lives; it *confirms*, or strengthens, our membership in the Church which began at Baptism.

Sacraments of initiation Baptism, Confirmation, and Eucharist are called sacraments of initiation (belonging) because they mark our membership in the Church.

Wisdom The gift of the Holy Spirit that helps us see God, ourselves, and others clearly—as God sees us.

begin to see and to know ourselves clearly . . . as God sees and knows us.

The gift of wisdom is like a built-in sense of balance, helping us measure the rightness or wrongness of things. In the light of wisdom, we're more likely to make choices that fit the goodness of God's plan—and when we make mistakes, we're more likely to face up to them honestly. The gift of wisdom helps us grow in self-esteem without going overboard, because we "see clearly" that everything we are and everything we can be comes from God.

Most of all, the gift of wisdom helps us look and listen for signs of God's care in our lives. In Maria's case, wisdom—the voice of the Spirit—comes through loud and clear in the words of her friend Shannon: "I will still be your friend, no matter what you decide."

Think It Over/Write About It

1. How would you describe your own identity right now? How do you think you will describe yourself ten years from now?
2. What are two or three things you do that show you are a Catholic?
3. How does the Holy Spirit's gift of wisdom make a difference in your life?

A Statement of Belief

One way that Catholics have expressed their identity throughout the ages is by praying the Apostles' Creed. The earliest Christians, who were baptized as adults, learned this prayer as part of preparing for the sacrament. Through the words of the Creed, Christians praise God and state their belief in Father, Son, and Holy Spirit. This *profession of faith* is another way of saying, "This is who we are, this is what is important to us."

You probably memorized the Apostles' Creed as a young child. Maybe the words were difficult to understand. But now, as you think about publicly confirming your Catholic identity, it's important to consider what the Creed really means.

The Apostles' Creed begins, "I believe in God, the Father almighty, Creator of heaven and earth." These words say that we believe *in* God: we put our trust and our lives in God's hands. They also say what we believe *about* God.

A Loving Father

When we pray the Creed, we are saying that God is good and loving. God rejoices in having given us life. God wants us to make wise decisions, but He understands when we fail. He is willing to forgive us time and again. In the Creed, we say that we believe God is the Creator of all things. God established times and seasons, and set up the rules by which all things come into being, grow, and change.

This first article, or statement, of the Creed also says something about what we believe about *ourselves.* When we pray the Creed, we are saying that we believe we are God's children. We are saying that all people are made in God's image and likeness—free to choose, to love, and to be loved. If we really believe what we are saying, we will see the worth and dignity in every person, and treat everyone with kindness and respect.

A Special Help

If we really believe . . . that's the challenge. Saying the words of the Creed over and over won't make us take them seriously. No one can *force* us to believe.

We can only meet this challenge with *faith.* Faith—like the fullness of the Spirit's gifts in Confirmation—comes to us from God. In a way, faith is the gift that works with all the others. It's a two-way gift: faith comes to us from God, in Baptism, and we return it, throughout our lives, by living what we believe.

We're not talking about "blind" faith, either. Instead, our faith is like a giant telescope that sees far beyond anything the unaided eye could uncover. At many times and in many ways, faith helps us get a glimpse of the goodness of God.

Faith works with the Holy Spirit's gift of wisdom to help us know the truth about ourselves and about God.

The Faith of Jesus

The gifts of faith and wisdom are clearly present in the life of Jesus. Jesus believed in God and trusted that God loved Him. Throughout His life, Jesus told others about this loving Father. In His teaching, He invited others to increase their faith in God's care.

"Do not worry about your life, what you will eat, or about your body, what you will wear," Jesus said. "Is not life more than food and the body more than clothing? Look at the birds in the sky; they do not sow or reap, they gather nothing into barns, yet your heavenly

Father feeds them. And are you not more important than birds? . . . If God so clothes the grass of the field, which grows today and is thrown into the fire tomorrow, will He not provide for you?" *(Matthew 6:25–33)*.

People today face the same challenge as those who first listened to Jesus. Nearly everyone finds it difficult, at times, to believe in a God who can't be seen. They find it hard to trust in God when things go wrong. They have trouble believing that God really does care for them individually.

Tough times, times of doubt, and hard-to-answer questions test the quality of a person's faith. People who can hold on to faith survive these times. Their faith grows stronger. One such person of faith was Patrick of Ireland.

Saint Patrick's Faith

"I hate you," Patrick thought to himself as Milchu, the Irish chieftain, continued to whip him.

"Do you promise not to run away again?" Milchu snarled.

"I promise," said young Patrick, wincing from the pain.

"All right then," Milchu said as he put down the whip. "Let's see if you're any good with sheep. But I warn you, if you lay a hand on them, I'll kill you, understand?"

Patrick nodded. His throat was choked with tears, and his back burned where the whip had cut him.

"Here's a loaf of bread," Milchu said gruffly. "I want to see you and the sheep back here in a week."

Patrick accepted the bread, grateful to be getting away from the cruel Milchu. Two years ago, he'd been kidnapped from his homeland by pirates, who took him to Ireland and sold him to Milchu as a slave.

Patrick led the sheep to a distant valley. He sat beside a stream and nibbled the loaf of bread, knowing it had to last a week. Hungry and hurt, Patrick stared at the running water and thought about home. He remembered a song his mother had sung.

"The Lord is my shepherd," Patrick sang quietly, but the words meant nothing to him.

The night grew cold, and a wolf howled in the distance. Patrick pulled his tattered cloak around him and looked up at the stars. He remembered a night long ago, when his father had told him that God created the stars.

"God, if You exist, I hope You're not like Milchu," Patrick said into the darkness. "If You exist, get me out of this terrible place!"

Over the years that followed, Patrick had time to think. He realized that he did not know God very well. For the first time in his life, he began to pray. And the more he prayed, the more clearly he saw God's care. "The love of God came to me more and more, and my faith was strengthened," Patrick wrote many years later. "I realized that God not only loved me, but the Irish people as well."

■ ■ ■

Religious Vocabulary

Profession of faith A public statement of belief. The *Creed* (a word which means "I believe") is our profession of faith.

Faith The virtue by which we put our trust in God and believe all that God has revealed, or made known, to us.

Trinity The mystery of three Divine Persons—Father, Son, and Holy Spirit—in one God.

After years of slavery, Patrick escaped and made his way home. He stayed only long enough to study for the priesthood and to be ordained. Then, Patrick returned to Ireland— the land of his captivity—to share his faith with the people he had once hated. Because of what they saw in Patrick, the Irish people believed in the *Trinity*, and became Catholics.

Think It Over/Write About It

1. How do you picture God?
2. How have you experienced that God loves you?
3. What do the words of Jesus and the story of Saint Patrick have to say to you about your own struggle to believe?

Making Faith Real

Every Catholic is faced with the same challenge as Patrick—to grow in faith and then to translate this faith into action. This challenge faces you as you prepare for Confirmation.

One part of the challenge is to "see" yourself as you really are, with your strengths and weaknesses. Complete the following sentences:

1. I feel good about myself because _____

_____

_____

2. Three things I can do well are _____

_____

_____

3. Three things I have trouble doing are _____

_____

_____

Another part of the challenge is to get to know God better—to trust in Him and believe in Him. Decide how you will meet this part of the challenge, and complete these promises:

1. One thing I will do this week to get to know God better is _____

_____

_____

2. One thing I will entrust to God's care this week is _____

_____

_____

3. One way I will show, this week, that I believe in God is _____

_____

_____

True or False

Circle the T if the statement is true. Circle the F if the statement is false.

1. People with high self-esteem think they are better than everyone else.   T   F
2. All people ask questions about their identity.   T   F
3. The three sacraments of initiation are Baptism, Eucharist, and Reconciliation.   T   F
4. The decision to be confirmed is a decision you have to make all alone.   T   F
5. The gift of wisdom helps us to see ourselves and others as God sees us.   T   F
6. Wisdom is a help in making good choices.   T   F
7. Only some people are made in God's image and likeness.   T   F
8. It is always easy to have faith.   T   F
9. The Apostles' Creed is a profession of faith.   T   F
10. Jesus taught His followers that God cares for every person.   T   F

Vocabulary Review

Look up each of the following words in the Glossary which begins on page 117. Then, make up a sentence using each word.

Baptism   creed   Trinity
Confirmation   faith   wisdom

1. _____
_____
2. _____
_____
3. _____
_____
4. _____
_____
5. _____
_____
6. _____
_____

Your Confirmation Name

Almost everyone has two names: a first name and a last name. Your first name tells others who you are. Your last name tells others what family you belong to.

Names are a sign of power. When you were baptized, all sin was forgiven *in the name of* the Father, of the Son, and of the Holy Spirit. You were given a "Christian" name—the name of one of the saints or heroes of the Bible, for example, who became your "patron." You can find many examples in the New Testament of the Apostles' curing and forgiving in the name of Jesus. And you probably remember Bible stories in which a person's name was changed to show that he or she had entered into a new relationship with God.

Your Confirmation is an opportunity to enter into a deeper relationship with God and with the Church. One Confirmation custom is to choose a new name to symbolize this relationship. This "Confirmation name" is used in the ceremony. You may even choose your baptismal name, if you like, because there is a close connection between Baptism and Confirmation.

Answer the following questions. Talk over your answers with your family, and use reference books if necessary.

1. What is your complete baptismal name?
2. Why did your parents give you these names?
3. What do these names mean?
4. What name do you like your friends to call you? Why?
5. What would you like your Confirmation name to be?
6. Why would you like this name? What does it mean to you?

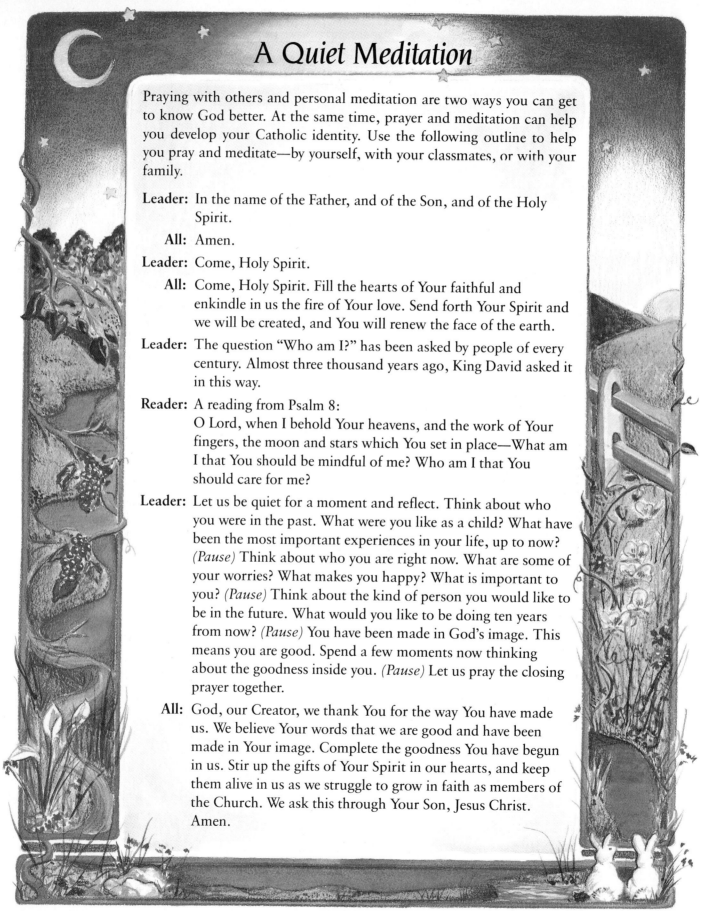

A Quiet Meditation

Praying with others and personal meditation are two ways you can get to know God better. At the same time, prayer and meditation can help you develop your Catholic identity. Use the following outline to help you pray and meditate—by yourself, with your classmates, or with your family.

Leader: In the name of the Father, and of the Son, and of the Holy Spirit.

All: Amen.

Leader: Come, Holy Spirit.

All: Come, Holy Spirit. Fill the hearts of Your faithful and enkindle in us the fire of Your love. Send forth Your Spirit and we will be created, and You will renew the face of the earth.

Leader: The question "Who am I?" has been asked by people of every century. Almost three thousand years ago, King David asked it in this way.

Reader: A reading from Psalm 8:
O Lord, when I behold Your heavens, and the work of Your fingers, the moon and stars which You set in place—What am I that You should be mindful of me? Who am I that You should care for me?

Leader: Let us be quiet for a moment and reflect. Think about who you were in the past. What were you like as a child? What have been the most important experiences in your life, up to now? *(Pause)* Think about who you are right now. What are some of your worries? What makes you happy? What is important to you? *(Pause)* Think about the kind of person you would like to be in the future. What would you like to be doing ten years from now? *(Pause)* You have been made in God's image. This means you are good. Spend a few moments now thinking about the goodness inside you. *(Pause)* Let us pray the closing prayer together.

All: God, our Creator, we thank You for the way You have made us. We believe Your words that we are good and have been made in Your image. Complete the goodness You have begun in us. Stir up the gifts of Your Spirit in our hearts, and keep them alive in us as we struggle to grow in faith as members of the Church. We ask this through Your Son, Jesus Christ. Amen.

2

The Jesus Story

In This Chapter

- You will explore the role of friendship in your own life.
- You will learn that knowledge, a gift of the Holy Spirit, can help you grow in friendship with Jesus.
- You will see that Bible study and prayer are two important ways Catholics come to know Jesus better.

The Challenge

- To grow in friendship with myself and others
- To grow in friendship with Jesus
- To prepare for Confirmation by choosing a sponsor

Old Friends

Arthur envied me because I got to ride to school every day with Heather Beeman. He was surprised when I told him it wasn't all that great.

Mrs. Beeman and my mom grew up together. It seemed like our families had been friends forever. When Heather and I were little kids, our families shared campsites on vacation. One time, I gave Heather a ride on the back of my brother's bike. I couldn't stand most of my mom's friends' kids, but I actually got along with Heather.

Not anymore, though. Our moms were still friends, but Heather and I went our separate ways when we started junior high school. The problem was ninth-grade boys. They liked Heather; they even bought her lunch. Ninth-grade boys didn't like me. They stole my lunch money and stuffed me into lockers.

Still, my friend Arthur thought it couldn't hurt to be seen with Heather on the way to school. Mom had arranged for Mrs. Beeman to drop us off on her way to work every morning.

"It's no use," I told Arthur. "Nobody's going to *see* me with Heather."

From the first week of junior high, Heather had set up some unspoken rules: she would get out of the car first. I would wait, and then walk—fast—in the other direction.

Once, Michelle de Martino, Heather's new best friend, met her by the curb. As they walked, Michelle pointed a thumb back at the car and asked Heather, "Who is *that*?"

"Oh, that's just Danny," Heather answered. "My mom has to drive him to school every day."

Arthur was starting to get the picture.

Things got even clearer on the afternoon of our first school dance. By the last hour, I knew that Arthur and I were the only boys who *hadn't* asked a girl to dance. I figured everybody else in the gym knew it, too.

With just a few minutes left before Mr. Aames (our principal-turned-DJ) stopped playing records, I came up with a great idea: I would ask Heather to dance!

"Danny, that's a rap song," Heather explained patiently, after I asked her. "We can't dance to that."

I guess I should have known better. The worst part was walking back across the gym floor to face Arthur and the other guys. For all they knew, Heather could have said, "Leave me alone, stupid." I told them I was going to dance with Heather later.

Later never came. The dance ended. I felt angry, embarrassed, and weird. And I blamed Heather Beeman.

Arthur, Joey Coca, and I walked slowly down Fountain Avenue, sharing the bad mood. About halfway home, we noticed

Heather, Michelle, and some other girls across the street. They were filling balloons with water from a garden faucet and throwing them at one another.

It looked like fun, but then an older woman came out on the porch and told the girls to stop it. Michelle started to talk back to the woman, and some of the other girls chimed in.

I watched Heather. She just stood there for a minute, and then she said something to Michelle. Michelle ignored her. Then, Heather cut across the street and headed right for us.

"Hi, Danny," she said.

I glanced at Arthur and Joey. Arthur was grinning, and Joey seemed impressed that Heather knew my name.

"Those girls are acting cold to that lady," Heather explained. "I don't like it. Is it OK if I walk home with you guys?"

As we walked on together, mostly in silence, I kept thinking of Heather standing there on the lawn, not joining in the teasing. "Heather's my friend," I was thinking, and, for the first time in weeks, it was a comfortable thought.

Think It Over/Write About It

1. How would you describe the friendship that Danny and Heather had as children? What changed their friendship?
2. Why did Danny blame Heather for his bad mood after the dance?
3. What new view of Heather does Danny have at the end of the story? What will happen to their friendship now?
4. Think about one of your own friendships. Write a paragraph or draw a chart that traces the changes and growth in your relationship.

Being a Friend

We learn about people by looking at the way they act. We learn about people by spending time with them, listening to their stories, and asking them questions. When we learn more about other people, we can begin to build friendships. Having friends makes life better.

Heather and Danny experienced one kind of friendship as children. This early friendship wasn't based on learning about each other; the two drifted together because their mothers were friends. In junior high school, Heather and Danny drifted apart. But then Danny learned something new about Heather by watching her behavior. She left her friends to walk with him. Each made a choice to spend time with the other—to talk, to learn, to listen. Now, their friendship has a chance to grow.

One of the most important qualities of friendship is knowledge. The more we know about a person's likes and dislikes and the kinds of things he or she can do, the better chance we have to form a friendship.

Worth Working For

Self-knowledge is an important part of friendship, too. We have to know about our own likes and dislikes. We have to learn what we are capable of doing. And we have to like what we learn about ourselves, because it's hard to care about others when we do not care about ourselves.

Time is another important part of developing friendships. It takes time to learn about ourselves and about others. As Danny learned about Heather, people act differently in different situations. First impressions can be deceiving: the person who seems conceited or snobby, for instance, may really be shy and afraid to begin a conversation. People who take the time to get to know others usually make the best friends.

Knowledge helps us see people as they really are. The people we get to know best can become our best friends—and such friendships are worth working for.

A Deeper Friendship

In Baptism and Confirmation, the Holy Spirit gives us a way to boost our natural knowledge of ourselves and others. The Spirit's *gift of knowledge* helps us to become better friends with God. Through the gift of knowledge, we are open to learning more about God in the Persons of Father, Son, and Holy Spirit. We are moved to examine what we've learned, prayerfully and lovingly.

Really knowing that God is a Friend is valuable and comforting. Knowing that God listens to us as we express our needs, fears, and joys helps us make better Christian choices. Knowing that God understands our feelings—even when we cannot put them into words—reassures us that we always have a good Listener.

The gift of knowledge answers one of our deepest longings—to be known. God the Father knows us as a loving Parent knows a child, proud of His creation yet respectful of our individuality. Jesus knows us as a Brother, ready to share with us our daily experiences. The Holy Spirit knows us as a gentle Guide, helping us see the good in ourselves and in others.

Saint Joseph's Knowledge

Saint Matthew's Gospel tells the story of how the gift of knowledge helped a special friendship. The story is about Mary, the Mother of Jesus, and Joseph, His foster father.

Although Mary and Joseph had made a sacred promise to be married, they probably did not know each other much better than any engaged couple of their time. Before the wedding day, Saint Matthew tells us, Joseph found out that Mary was pregnant. According to the laws of those days, Joseph could have turned Mary over to the authorities to be stoned to death.

■ ■ ■

Religious Vocabulary

The gift of knowledge The gift of the Holy Spirit that helps us know—and be known by—God, ourselves, and others in a deeper way.

Jesus The name given to the Second Person of the Trinity, the Son of God. Jesus is both God and man. The name "Jesus" means "God saves His people."

Messiah A Hebrew word that means "the anointed (or chosen) one," the Savior God promised to His People. We believe that Jesus is the promised Messiah. The name "Christ" is the Greek form of "Messiah."

Joseph did not want this to happen. He cared for Mary very much. To protect her good name, Joseph decided to break off their engagement privately. But then, Joseph received the gift of knowledge.

In a dream, an angel spoke to Joseph: "Do not be afraid to take Mary as your wife. For it is through the Holy Spirit that this child has been conceived in her. She will bear a son and you are to name Him *Jesus*, because He will save His people from their sins" *(Matthew 1:20–21)*.

Joseph thought about his dream. He remembered that the prophet Isaiah had predicted the birth of a *Messiah*—the Savior promised by God. Joseph acted on the knowledge he had received. Instead of judging Mary by the law, he responded with love. Joseph married Mary, and became the foster father of her Son—whom he named Jesus.

Scripture calls Joseph "a just man." This title is used for those who are holy, who know God well. The Spirit's gift of knowledge increased Joseph's own knowledge of and love for Mary. Joseph's openness to that gift made a wonderful difference in his life . . . and changed the course of history forever.

Think It Over/Write About It

1. Think about your own friendships. How important were the qualities of knowledge and time in forming your friendships?
2. How can learning more about God help you make better Christian choices?
3. How did the gift of knowledge help Joseph be a better friend to Mary?
4. What difference does the Spirit's gift of knowledge make in your life?

Growing in Knowledge

Thomas was puzzled. He had spent the entire morning looking for Albert, and couldn't find him anywhere. Finally, Thomas came upon Albert sitting in the garden.

"What's wrong with this essay I wrote?" Thomas asked his friend and teacher. "Why did you give me such a poor mark?"

Albert continued to stare at the flowers. "Tell me what you see here," he said, after a few moments.

Thomas looked around quickly. "Roses," he answered.

"And what are they doing?" Albert asked.

"Why, they're doing what every flower does," Thomas answered, impatiently. "They're doing nothing."

"Wrong," Albert smiled. He bent toward the rosebush and pointed. "This one here is providing shelter for a caterpillar's cocoon. And this one is feeding a bee."

Thomas looked closer, and saw that what Albert said was true.

"And what is that hummingbird doing?" Albert pointed up.

"Flying," Thomas answered.

"Only partially correct," Albert responded. "Unlike any of the other birds in the garden, it is flying *backward*."

Once again Thomas realized that Albert was right. "But what does this have to do with my essay?" he asked.

Albert motioned for Thomas to sit beside him on the bench. "You don't really know this garden because you don't spend time here," Albert explained. "In the same way, your paper showed me that you know many things *about* Jesus' life and teachings, but you do not really know Jesus."

"Then teach me," Thomas replied.

So Albert began to teach Thomas to pray. At first, nothing seemed different. But one day, Thomas felt the presence of Jesus in his heart. He sensed that Jesus was very near him, asking to be his Friend.

After that, Thomas talked with Jesus in many ways. Sometimes, he prayed quietly in his room, or read the Scriptures in the garden. Sometimes, he talked to Jesus at Mass. He spent many hours before the *Blessed Sacrament*.

Thomas shared his newfound knowledge with others. He wrote volumes of *theology* and composed beautiful Church music. In all of his works there is the sense of friendship with God, rooted in knowledge and faith. The Church calls Thomas Aquinas one of the greatest of saints.

Faith is especially important when the Person we are trying to get to know is Jesus. Jesus is not just an ordinary friend. He lived and died many years ago. What makes Jesus so special is that He also rose from the dead, and remains alive and with us today. We need the eyes of faith to come to know Jesus where we meet Him now: in the Eucharist, in Scripture, and in the hearts of all believers.

As Catholic Christians, we proclaim our knowledge of Jesus in the words of the Creed: "I believe in Jesus Christ, God's only Son, our Lord. He was conceived by the power of the Holy Spirit, and born of the Virgin Mary." At the same time, we proclaim our lifelong need to know *more* about Jesus—the Friend who came to teach us how to love not just our friends, but our enemies as well.

Why Know Jesus?

As the *Gospels* tell us, knowing Jesus offers us a number of real advantages. The first benefit is that, in Jesus, we have a Friend who will never leave us. "I will always be with you," Jesus promised *(Matthew 28:20)*. "I will not leave you orphans," Jesus told His friends before He died *(John 14:18)*.

A second advantage is that the more we know Jesus, the more we learn about how to be a friend to others. "Love your neighbor as you love yourself," Jesus taught *(Matthew 22:39)*. Jesus knew that real friends share one another's cares and joys. He knew that people grow in friendship when they spend time together, share experiences, and listen to one another.

Jesus Himself went out of His way to make people feel welcome. He had many friends who were considered outcasts: tax collectors, prostitutes, public sinners. Jesus made them feel welcomed and accepted—and, in turn, they welcomed Him into their lives.

Jesus once described Himself as a vine. He called His friends the branches. "Remain in Me, and you will bear much fruit," Jesus said *(John 15:5)*. When we are friends with Jesus, we can be the people God calls us to be. We can become our best selves as part of His life-giving vine.

Faith and Knowledge

"Teach me," Thomas Aquinas begged his friend, Albert. As you prepare for Confirmation, you can look to others—your teacher, your pastor, your family, the person you will choose as a sponsor—to help you grow in faith and knowledge of Jesus. The ways of getting to know Jesus that Saint Albert recommended to Thomas can help you, too.

1. You can study the Bible. The Bible is like a scrapbook containing "snapshots" from the life of Jesus. The Old Testament tells about the people who came before Jesus and awaited His birth. The New Testament shows us specific events in the life of Jesus, and the impact His teachings had on His friends and followers.

Through Bible study, you can learn more about the real Jesus—what He was like, how He related to others, what His words mean. Getting to know Jesus in this way is just like getting to know a friend. There is always something new and interesting to discover.

2. You can pray. Prayer is like a conversation. Sometimes, you talk and Jesus listens. Sometimes, Jesus speaks and you listen. You can share your happy times and even your tears with Jesus. You can pray in thanksgiving for the wonder of being alive, or ask for help in the darkest times.

Regardless of what form your prayer takes, it is helping you to build a lasting friendship with Jesus. What you learn from Jesus in prayer can help you be a better friend to yourself and to others.

■ ■ ■

Religious Vocabulary

Blessed Sacrament The name for Jesus Christ truly present in the Eucharist. In every church, the Blessed Sacrament—in the form of Hosts consecrated at Mass—is kept in the tabernacle. A lamp burns before the tabernacle at all times, to remind us of the presence of Jesus.

Theology A word that means "the study of God." Theologians (like Saint Thomas Aquinas) devote their lives to learning about God and about our faith. Guided by the teaching authority of the pope and the bishops, theology helps us to know God.

Gospels The accounts of Jesus' life and teachings found in the New Testament of the Bible. There are four Gospels, named for their traditional authors: Saint Matthew, Saint Mark, Saint Luke, and Saint John. The word "gospel" means "good news."

Knowing Jesus

With the help of his teacher, Saint Albert the Great, Saint Thomas Aquinas grew in the Holy Spirit's gift of knowledge. His relationship with Jesus grew from an intellectual study to a personal friendship. That growth could only take place with faith.

Faith works with the Spirit's gift of knowledge to move us beyond the surface details. Another way to describe this faith-filled knowledge is "insight." When we see with the eyes of faith, we have insight into ourselves: We know why we do what we do. Faith and knowledge give us the insight to find friendships in unlikely places. We get a glimpse of the goodness in another person, and we are more willing to work to get to know that person better.

Think It Over/Write About It

1. How did Saint Thomas Aquinas grow in his knowledge of Jesus?
2. How does faith work with the Holy Spirit's gift of knowledge?
3. What is one advantage of friendship with Jesus? How can getting to know Jesus help you be a better friend?
4. Compose your own short prayer to Jesus. Include one or two questions you want to ask Him, and one way you would like to grow in friendship.

Knowledge Makes a Difference

Imagine that you and your friends are at a fast-food restaurant after school. In the corner of the room, you notice a girl sitting all by herself. You recognize her as a new student in your class. You talked to her once, but she didn't seem very friendly.

How do you feel about the girl?

_____

_____

Now, unscramble the following sentences to learn more about the girl:

E H S / S I / R Y E V / H Y S / D N A /

__ __ __/__ __/__ __ __ __/__ __ __/__ __ __/

A R F A D I / F O / E W N / E E P P L O .

__ __ __ __ __ __/__ __/__ __ __/__ __ __ __ __ .

H E S / S E D O / N T O / K E S P A /

__ __ __/__ __ __ __ __/__ __ __/__ __ __ __ __/

H I S L E G N .

__ __ __ __ __ __ __ .

E S H / S I / O G D O / T A / R O S C E C .

__ __ __/__ __/__ __ __ __/__ __/__ __ __ __ __ __ .

How do you feel about the girl after learning these additional facts?

_____

_____

Will this additional knowledge make a difference in the way you act toward the girl from now on? Why or why not?

_____

_____

Write one thing you will do this week to learn more about:

Yourself _____

Others _____

Jesus _____

Making Connections

Match the terms in Column B with the descriptions in Column A.
Write the correct letter on each line.

_____ 1. Albert's student and friend, who became a great saint.

_____ 2. A conversation with Jesus.

_____ 3. A close, personal relationship that grows through time and knowledge.

_____ 4. The gift of the Holy Spirit that works with faith to help us learn about God.

_____ 5. Along with knowledge, this is an important quality of friendship.

_____ 6. Thomas' teacher and friend.

_____ 7. The study of God.

_____ 8. The Second Person of the Trinity, the Messiah.

_____ 9. Learning about Jesus by reading the Scriptures.

_____10. The Real Presence of Jesus Christ in the Eucharist.

a. knowledge
b. Saint Albert the Great
c. time
d. theology
e. Blessed Sacrament
f. Saint Thomas Aquinas
g. Bible study
h. friendship
i. Jesus
j. prayer

Vocabulary Review

Look up each of the following words in the Glossary which begins on page 117. Then, write a short paragraph that uses all of these words.

Gospels	knowledge	prayer
Jesus Christ	Messiah	Son of God

_____

_____

_____

_____

_____

_____

_____

Choosing a Sponsor

A *sponsor* is someone who walks with you on the journey of faith leading to Confirmation. Your sponsor is a special kind of friend, one who shares with you his or her own faith, knowledge, and experience of being a Christian.

During the rite (or ceremony) of Confirmation, your sponsor will present you to the bishop and to the community, as a sign of your readiness to receive the sacrament. Your relationship with your sponsor does not end with the ceremony, however; he or she has the important task of continuing to help you as you grow in faith.

You choose your own sponsor for Confirmation. Your sponsor should be someone who has already had a good influence on your life in the Church. You may choose one of your baptismal godparents to sponsor you for Confirmation, or any other adult who is a practicing Catholic.

The duties of a sponsor are:

• to stand with you at the Confirmation ceremony;
• to present you to the bishop and the community;
• to be willing to help you live as a follower of Jesus.

A sponsor must be:

• a Catholic who has received the sacraments of Baptism, Eucharist, and Confirmation;
• sufficiently mature to guide and assist you in your faith.

Before the next class, think about the person you would like to choose as your Confirmation sponsor. Talk over your decision with your family, if you wish. When you have asked your sponsor, and he or she has agreed, fill out the following information, and sign the page together.

My Confirmation sponsor will be: _____
(Name)

I would especially like my sponsor to help me with _____

_____

_____   _____
(Your Signature)   (Sponsor's Signature)

Wisdom and Knowledge

Wisdom and knowledge are two important gifts of the Holy Spirit. Use the outline on this page to help you pray for openness to these gifts in your life. You can pray by yourself, with your classmates, or with your family.

Scripture Readings (Choose 1 or 2):
Psalm 8:1–10 (Creation reveals God's wisdom)
Psalm 139:1–18, 23–24 (God made us and knows us)
Romans 11:33–36 (The wisdom and knowledge of God)
Philippians 3:7–14 (To know Christ Jesus)

Music: Choose a hymn, song, or piece of instrumental music that has meaning for you—one that speaks to the theme of your prayer. Sing or listen to the music.

Sharing Experience: Think about a time when you have experienced the gifts of wisdom or knowledge. If you are praying with others, share your experience.

Prayer: Read the following petitions aloud. If you are in a group, take turns reading the petitions. After each petition, pray: "Lord, give us wisdom, and help us to know You better."
Whenever we feel we are not "good enough" . . .
Whenever we try to do what is right . . .
Whenever we are afraid to speak up for others . . .
Whenever we feel sad or lonely . . .
Whenever we meet someone who is "different" . . .
Whenever we reach out to others with kindness and friendship . . .
Then, pray this prayer together:
Lord, we have many needs. Give us the wisdom to see You more clearly. Give us the knowledge to love You more dearly. And give us the faith to follow You more nearly, day by day. Amen.

The Meaning of Eucharist

In This Chapter

- You will reflect on the respect you have for yourself, for others, and for God.
- You will learn the meaning of reverence, a gift of the Holy Spirit.
- You will see that one important way Catholics practice the gift of reverence is by participation in the Eucharist.

The Challenge

- To respect others, and to believe that I am worthy of respect
- To see that the gift of reverence has a place in my life
- To come to the Eucharist as a willing, active participant

Charlie and Saint Betty

In the weeks before Christmas, Charlie's teacher talked about Advent promises. "Think of some ways you can show your love for Jesus," she challenged the students.

Charlie thought his teacher's suggestion was a good one. He considered a few possibilities, but rejected each one. Finally, Charlie decided to visit the church each day and pray for a few minutes. He figured it was a simple enough promise—he could cut through the church on his way to the bus stop.

There was another reason for Charlie's promise. Ever since he was a little boy, Charlie had been fascinated by the sight of the red lamp that burned day and night in front of the tabernacle. "The lamp reminds us that Jesus is present in the Blessed Sacrament," Charlie's mother had explained to him when he

asked. Even now, Charlie felt a special, peaceful feeling in the presence of the Blessed Sacrament—especially when the church was quiet and almost empty.

Charlie began his plan on a Monday. Football practice ended a little after 4 o'clock. Charlie slung his cleats over his shoulder, brushed the brown grass off his socks, and practically tiptoed into the church. He knelt down in the last row of pews.

"Now, what do I do?" Charlie wondered. He thought he should pray, so he began whispering the Lord's Prayer. But his thoughts kept wandering back to football practice, to his science project that was due on Friday. . . .

It was no use. Charlie decided to leave—after all, he'd only promised to spend a minute or two in church. But as he stood up, he rattled the kneeler and the noise echoed like a firecracker.

That's when Charlie noticed her—the old woman who spent hours and hours in church—turning to face him from her seat across the aisle. The kids in school called her "Saint Betty—because all she does is pray." Some kids even mocked her behind her back.

Charlie hurried out of the church. He didn't notice that Saint Betty had gotten up, too, and was following him out the front door.

"Hey, boy! You forgot your shoes," Saint Betty said to Charlie, when she caught up to him at the bus stop.

"Thank you," Charlie gulped. Then he turned and pretended to look down the street for the bus. Out of the corner of his eye, Charlie saw Betty cross the street and enter the retirement home.

For the next three days, the two were the only people in church after four o'clock. On Wednesday, Charlie spent all of his "prayer" time wondering how Betty could sit in church for so long. He knew that Betty always attended the early-morning weekday Mass. Did she stay *all day*?

On Friday, Betty joined Charlie at the bus bench. "I go to my sister's house on weekends," she said, even though Charlie hadn't asked.

But since Betty had broken the silence, there was one question Charlie couldn't resist. "How can you pray so long?" he blurted out. "What do you pray about?"

"Oh, I don't pray *about* anything," she answered. "I just let Jesus share my thoughts. And I let Him look at me—just another one of His Father's children."

Betty's answer made Charlie feel better. He'd started to wonder if he'd wasted his week of prayer. He'd never once gotten through a whole rosary, and after the first day or two he'd given up on repeating any of the prayers he knew by heart. Instead, Charlie had just "thought about things," the way Saint Betty said she did.

"Can I ask you a question?" Betty interrupted Charlie's thoughts. "Why do *you* come to church every day?"

Charlie explained that he was preparing for Confirmation. He told Betty about his teacher's suggestion for Advent promises. Then, he introduced himself.

"I'm Charlie, by the way," he said, holding out his hand.

The old woman's handshake was surprisingly firm. "Nice to meet you," she said. My name is Rebecca Sprigg."

Saint Betty wasn't a saint after all. She wasn't even a Betty!

As Rebecca started across the street, Charlie called after her. "My class is having a meeting next week, with parents and sponsors," he said. "The meeting's about prayer. Would you . . . want to come, too?"

Think It Over/Write About It

1. How did Charlie and Rebecca show respect for each other?
2. What do you think Rebecca meant when she said that part of her prayer was just "letting Jesus look at her"? What would Jesus see if He looked at you?
3. Before he listened to Rebecca, why did Charlie feel he might have wasted his prayer time?
4. Write a sequel to the story. What do you think happens at the class meeting?

A Second Look

Charlie and Rebecca both came to church expecting to find God. They didn't expect to find each other. Rebecca could have been annoyed by a teenage boy in dirty football socks, thumping around in a back pew. Charlie might have turned away from being seen with a woman whose behavior seemed odd to his friends.

Negative attitudes can ruin an experience. Charlie and Rebecca didn't let negative attitudes affect their time in church. Instead, they respected each other's right to be there.

Respect—the quality of honoring yourself and others—literally means "to take a second look." When Charlie and Rebecca refused to see each other as stereotypes—the noisy teenager, the funny old lady—they were showing respect. By the end of their week together, Charlie cared enough about Rebecca to invite her to the class meeting. And *Rebecca* cared enough about Charlie to tell him her real name!

Worthy of Respect

At this time in your life, you're probably reminded often of the respect that you owe to others—your parents, your teachers, those in authority, older people. Respect may seem like a one-way street, an obligation you owe others without receiving anything in return.

But real respect is always mutual. It revolves around the idea of the *common good*—what is best for all involved. The common good of families is served when children respect parents by showing courtesy and following family rules, but also when parents respect their children by allowing them opportunities to grow in love and responsibility.

Any community—a classroom, a neighborhood, a nation, the Church—works best only when there is mutual respect. In a way, respect is a new way of looking at *obedience*. When we obey, we submit our will to the needs of another. We do so freely—or it would not be obedience, but slavery.

If we find ourselves thinking that respect is something that has to be *earned*, we end up seeing it as a limited quality, with only so much to go around. In reality, respect breeds respect. When you respect yourself (take a "second look" at the goodness within you), you are more likely to respect others—and to be found worthy of their respect.

The Gift of Reverence

There is a gift of the Holy Spirit that adds a new dimension to the natural gift of respect. This gift widens and deepens our respect toward God and all the people and things that God has made. It is *the gift of reverence*.

Reverence is a special way of responding to the goodness, beauty, and holiness of God. When we practice the gift of reverence, we are acknowledging, or recognizing, that God is the Source of all life and love. And, like all the Spirit's gifts, reverence moves us to action. Recognizing the goodness of God, we respond in prayer and worship. Recognizing that we ourselves are made in the image of God's goodness, we cherish the life within us—doing our best not to tarnish that image through carelessness or sin. Recognizing that all people are children of God, we act with respect, protecting human life in all its forms and working for justice and peace. And recognizing that creation itself—the world around us, with all its natural wonders—reflects God's goodness, we act with reverence to protect and care for our earthly home.

The Reverence of Jesus

The gift of reverence played an important part in the way Jesus treated others. One day, Jesus saw Zacchaeus perched up in a tree, struggling to get a look at Him. Most people did not like Zacchaeus because he was a tax collector. They also made fun of him because he

- - -

Religious Vocabulary

Respect The quality of honoring others, putting their needs before our own.

Common good The principle of doing what is best for all involved.

Obedience The free submission of one's will to another. Obedience is a virtue, or positive spiritual quality, when we obey out of love, respect, and the desire to do what is right.

The gift of reverence The gift of the Holy Spirit that moves us to show respect for God and for all the people and things God has made.

On another occasion, some parents tried to bring their children forward in the crowd so that Jesus could bless them. The disciples began to turn them away, thinking the children were a distraction. But Jesus said, "Let the little children come to Me," and He welcomed them *(Matthew 19:13–15)*.

Jesus even showed respect for lepers, who were feared and scorned by most people because of their contagious, disfiguring skin disease. When a leper approached Jesus, He did not turn away. Instead, Jesus spoke to the man and even touched him, forgiving his sins and curing the disease. After this encounter, Scripture tells us that Jesus went off to a quiet place to pray *(Luke 5:12–16)*, clearly expressing the connection between reverence for others and reverence for God.

was short. But Jesus reached out. "Zacchaeus, come down from there!" Jesus said. "I would like to eat dinner with you" *(Luke 19:1–10)*.

In all His actions, Jesus showed us that reverence involves both attitudes and behavior. The Holy Spirit's gift of reverence is not some distant, difficult virtue meant only for the "Saint Bettys" in our lives. It is a gift we can use and practice every day.

Think It Over/Write About It

1. How do you feel when you are asked to show respect for others?
2. Do you consider yourself someone worthy of respect? Why or why not?
3. Describe another example of the reverence Jesus showed to His Father and to others.
4. Think of a situation in your life that calls for the gift of reverence. Tell how your cooperation with this gift could make a difference.

An Attitude of Worship

Since the beginning of time, people have shown reverence to God through acts of *worship*. The Book of Genesis tells the story of Cain and Abel, two brothers with different attitudes toward worship. Cain grudgingly sacrificed, or offered to God, the leftover grain and fruit from his harvest. Abel, on the other hand, chose the finest first-born lamb from his flock to offer to the Lord in thanksgiving. The Lord accepted Abel's sacrifice, because it showed a sincere spirit of reverence. But because Cain was only "going through the motions" of worship, the Lord rejected his offering *(Genesis 4:2–5)*.

The Gospel of Luke records a similar story Jesus told about prayer. Two men, He explained, went to the Temple to pray. The first man spent his prayer time praising himself and complaining about the sins of others. The second man, an outcast from society, stood humbly and begged for God's mercy. "I tell you," Jesus said, "that the second man went home justified" *(Luke 18:9–14)*.

We can see that reverence is not only a gift, but an attitude that we bring to our own prayer and worship. This attitude of reverence is shown most clearly in the way we approach the greatest act of worship, the *Eucharist*.

Giving Thanks

The word "Eucharist" comes from a Greek word which means "to give thanks." When we gather for Mass, we are joined with other Catholics—in our own parish community, and all around the world—in one reverent act of thanksgiving.

The reason for giving thanks to God is found in the words of the Apostles' Creed (and in the similar wording of the *Nicene Creed*, or Profession of Faith, that we proclaim together after the Gospel is read at Mass). "I believe in Jesus Christ. . . . He suffered under Pontius Pilate, was crucified, died, and was buried. He descended to the dead. On the third day He rose again. He ascended into heaven, and is seated at the right hand of the Father. He will come again to judge the living and the dead."

In these very simple words we find the whole core of our Christian beliefs. Jesus, God's own Son, lived the gift of reverence as no other person has, offering His whole life to God. His *sacrifice* on the cross, which we celebrate and share in at every Mass, was an act of total respect, obedience, and thanksgiving. Because of His saving action, Jesus was able to restore the lines of communication between God and His people that had been broken by sin. Jesus not only pointed the way to His Father—He Himself *became* the Way.

In the Eucharist, we receive this same Son of God in Holy Communion. We accept into our own lives the reverence, obedience, and thankfulness of Jesus—and we are strengthened.

The Power of the Eucharist

"Sister Clare! Sister Clare! We are being attacked!"

The frightened voice startled Clare out of her prayer. She rose from the stone floor of the convent chapel in Assisi, Italy, where she had been kneeling for hours. Her sister, Agnes, stood with a crowd of villagers at the chapel door.

"The soldiers of the Saracen have almost reached the village," Agnes cried. "They will burn the town and kill us all!"

Though frightened herself, Sister Clare sprang into action. "Ring the bells at once," she told Agnes. "Tell the people to gather in the church."

Clare found Father Antonio, the village priest. As soon as the nuns and the villagers were safely gathered in the church, Father Antonio began to celebrate the Mass.

Throughout the *liturgy*, Sister Clare prayed for God's protection. When it was time for Communion, she went determinedly to the altar to receive the Body of Christ. In those days, people rarely received Communion, because they felt unworthy. But Clare had a deep reverence for the Eucharist and a deep reverence for herself. She received Communion often, and encouraged the other sisters to do so, as well.

After Mass, Clare spoke to Father Antonio. She asked him to bring the Blessed Sacrament to the convent chapel of San Damiano, where she lived. "If we put our trust in the Lord, and spend time with Him, I know the soldiers will not attack us," Sister Clare said firmly.

All night long, Clare knelt on the cold stone floor before the sacred Host. And in the morning, a messenger arrived from the village.

"The soldiers have turned back!" he cried. "We are saved!"

Filled with joy, the townspeople and the sisters prayed in thanksgiving. For Sister Clare, their miraculous escape was just one more sign of what she believed in all along: the saving power of the Eucharist.

Faith and Reverence

Today, we know Sister Clare as Saint Clare of Assisi, the friend of Saint Francis. Our time is very different from hers. The people of Clare's day thought that reverence meant praising

God from afar. They believed they were unworthy of drawing near to holy things. Having lost sight of God's love and mercy, they held themselves back from participation in the Mass and the reception of Communion.

We can make the opposite mistake today, when Catholics tend to receive Communion frequently and there are so many opportunities for being involved in the Mass. We can take the Eucharist for granted.

Faith works with the gift of reverence to help us find a balance. Faith helps us avoid the mistake of the first man in the Temple, who bragged about his own holiness, and the mistake of Cain, who merely "went through the motions" of worshiping God.

We need faith to understand that God loves us even when we are unworthy, and invites us to the sacraments. We need faith to recognize that our obligation to attend Mass is not a burden or a bore.

As you prepare for Confirmation, remember that another name for the gift of reverence is *piety*, which means "faithful

■ ■ ■

Religious Vocabulary

Worship The act of showing reverence and honor to God.

Eucharist The sacrament which celebrates Jesus' saving action, and in which we share His Body and Blood. We celebrate this sacrament in the Mass. The word "Eucharist" means "thanksgiving."

Nicene Creed The profession of faith that we proclaim at Mass. The words of this prayer, which are based on the earlier Apostles' Creed, were developed at Church councils in Nicaea and Constantinople, around the 4th century A.D.

Sacrifice An offering given to God, or something given up for the good of another. Jesus' suffering and death are the greatest sacrifice.

Liturgy A public act of worship, including formal prayers and actions. The Mass is the highest form of liturgy.

Piety Another name for the gift of reverence; a word that means "faithful obedience and love."

obedience and love." Piety is the response of Jesus to His Father. It is our response to God.

And remember, too, that God does not *need* our worship and honor. God is perfectly and completely happy as He is. By offering reverence to God at Mass, by receiving Communion, we are really doing something for *ourselves*. Because of God's goodness, we feel special. We feel loved. Because of God's goodness, we are protected and filled with power. In offering our reverence to God, we understand more clearly that we are God's children.

Think It Over/Write About It

1. Why did God accept the sacrifice of Abel and listen to the prayer of the humble man in the Temple?
2. In what way is Jesus' sacrifice on the cross a sign of reverence?
3. What do we celebrate in the Eucharist?
4. Think about your own attitudes toward prayer and worship. What would you like to change or improve about your attitudes?

Growing in Reverence

The Holy Spirit's gift of reverence, given in Baptism and brought to fullness in Confirmation, builds on the natural gifts of respect and obedience. You can grow in this gift of the Spirit by developing your own potential for reverent action.

   Read the project descriptions below. Choose and complete one of the projects. Share what you have learned with your classmates.

1. Read about the life of a saint or a contemporary Catholic hero. How did this person show reverence for himself or herself? For others? For creation? For God? Write a report on your findings.

2. Read two of the Eucharistic prayers used at Mass. (You will find these printed in the parish missal.) How are these prayers similar? How are they different? Compare and contrast the two prayers in a report or chart.

3. Without being asked, do three chores at home. (You might try doing chores that you usually find difficult or boring.) What was your family's reaction? How did your efforts make you feel? Write about it in a brief summary.

4. Spend some time in your parish church each day for a week. Keep a prayer journal recording your thoughts and meditations.

Fill in the Blanks

Complete the sentences below by filling in the correct word or phrase. Try to complete this exercise without looking back at the chapter.

1. The Book of _____ tells the story of two brothers, Cain and Abel. _____ offered his finest first-born lamb to God; _____ grudgingly offered some grain and fruit.

2. The quality of _____, or showing _____ to others, opens the way to other positive attitudes. It is important to show _____ to ourselves as well as to our parents, teachers, and all in authority.

3. From the beginning of time, people have _____ God.

4. _____ is the gift of the Holy Spirit that helps us show special love, respect, and obedience to God and to all the people and things God has made.

5. For Catholics, the highest act of worship is the sacrament of the _____, celebrated in the _____. At Mass, we celebrate the _____ of Jesus, and we share His Body and Blood by receiving _____.

6. Another name for the gift of reverence is _____, which means "faithful love and obedience."

Vocabulary Review

Look up each of the following words in the Glossary which begins on page 117. Then, choose two words and use them in original sentences.

Eucharistic prayer   liturgy
Holy Communion   worship

1. _____

   _____

2. _____

   _____

The Mass

The celebration of Confirmation—like that of Baptism—normally takes place during the Mass. This is a reminder that the sacraments are not separate moments, but part of our lives within the community of faith. At your Confirmation Mass, the bishop will call you forward to be anointed after the homily. The Scripture readings, prayers, and songs of the Mass will reflect the theme of the Holy Spirit's presence in your life.

You can prepare for Confirmation (and for your lifelong growth in faith) right now, by deepening your appreciation of and participation in the Mass. Here are some suggestions; try one or two each time you go to Mass in the upcoming weeks. Talk over your experiences with your sponsor and your family.

- *Prepare for each Mass.* If possible, you should look over the Scripture readings ahead of time (you can find them in the missalette). Spend a few moments before Mass asking for God's help and recalling the needs you wish to bring to God in prayer.
- *Listen to the readings.* God speaks to you, here and now, in the words of Scripture. The homily or sermon helps "break open" God's Word for you.
- *Respond in prayer and song.* You should be familiar with the common prayers of the Mass, so that you can respond clearly and with understanding. Singing is another way to pray at Mass. Don't be afraid to sing out, because the Mass is not a concert.
- *Make an offering.* Offer yourself to God as the gifts of bread and wine are presented. You may choose to work or save in order to make a monetary contribution to the needs of the parish, but there are gifts of time and service to others that you can offer, as well.
- *Receive Holy Communion.* This is the most important act of participation in the Mass. Receiving the Eucharist joins you to Jesus and to all those who believe in Him. Take time after receiving Communion to pray in thanksgiving.
- *Be a part of the parish community.* Reach out at the Sign of Peace. Instead of rushing off when the Mass is over, stay to talk to the priest and other parishioners. If you can, try to meet one new person each time you go to Mass.

Finding God's Love

Contemplation is the word we use for prayer and meditation that is focused on experiencing the presence of God. Our Judeo-Christian tradition is full of rich advice on practicing contemplation. Read and reflect on the passages below. Then, write your own brief meditation on how you experience God's presence.

God says to us, as to Moses, "Take off your shoes"—in other words, put aside the everyday things that "cover" you—and you will recognize that the place you are standing on right now is holy ground. For there is no part of life in which we cannot find the holiness of God *(Hasidic Jewish saying)*.

If My people, upon whom My name has been pronounced, humble themselves and pray, and seek My presence and turn from their evil ways, I will hear them from heaven and pardon their sins and revive their land *(2 Chronicles 7:14)*.

God's love for us is not greater in heaven than it is at this moment *(Saint Thomas Aquinas)*.

God, give me an open heart to find You everywhere, to glimpse the heaven enfolded in nature, and to experience eternity in the smallest act of love *(Thomas Merton)*.

If, Lord, Your love for me is so strong as to bind me to You—what holds me from You, Lord, for so long? What holds You, Lord, so long from me? *(Saint Teresa of Avila)*.

My Meditation

_____

_____

_____

4

To Love and Serve

In This Chapter

- You will think about the things that make people afraid.
- You will learn that courage, a gift of the Holy Spirit, helps break down the walls of fear that keep people from sharing and caring.
- You will see that the sacrament of Confirmation and the presence of the Holy Spirit strengthen Catholics for love and service.

The Challenge

- To face my fears—especially those that keep me from reaching out to others
- To believe that the Holy Spirit is with me, giving me courage and power
- To develop my skills and talents for serving others

No Longer Afraid

"I c-can't do it-t," Matt said in frustration. "Everyone w-will laugh at-t m-me."

"But if you don't give the oral report, you'll fail the class," Mrs. Johnson argued once again.

Mrs. Johnson was Matt's speech therapist. She had been working with him for over a year now on his stuttering problem.

"B-But I d-don't know what t-to t-talk about," Matt said.

"Tell them about what we do," Mrs. Johnson suggested. "Tell them about all the progress you've made."

"You mean t-tell them about-t all the hard-d *work*," Matt grinned.

"That, too," Mrs. Johnson said. "You write the report, and I'll practice it with you."

Reluctantly, Matt put his experiences on paper. Over and over, he practiced reading the report to Mrs. Johnson, until he had the words memorized. But even knowing his report by heart didn't make Matt feel any more confident about being able to speak in front of his classmates. Mrs. Johnson tried to reassure him—but she wouldn't be the one facing the laughter.

On the morning the report was due, Matt was the last student to be called on. The teasing began even before he opened his mouth. As Matt stood at his desk, Russell Ornelas, who sat next to him, hissed a loud whisper. "G-G-G-Good luck, M-M-M-Matthew," Russell stuttered.

Pretending to gather his notes, Matt casually shoved Russell's books to the floor. It wasn't a great move, but it made Matt feel better for a second or two.

He began his report slowly. "Most-t p-people t-take words for g-granted," Matt said. "I d-don't.

"Most p-people are afraid t-to speak in public," he continued. "I'm afraid t-to speak all the t-time."

Then he began to tell the class about his work with Mrs. Johnson, and all the ways she helped him. "M-My favorite exercise is m-music," Matt said. "M-Mrs. J-Johnson has me sing the words instead of s-saying them. There's something about-t music that relaxes m-me. When I s-sing the words, they come out right-t."

Matt stopped. He leaned down and dug into his backpack. Some kids began to giggle nervously, thinking Matt was too afraid to go on. But he surprised them.

From his backpack, Matt took a small cassette player. He popped in a cassette and pushed a button, and the classroom was filled with a familiar tune. It was an instrumental version of a really popular song. Matt began to sing with the music, as he had practiced with Mrs. Johnson. His voice was confident and strong—and he didn't stutter. When he had finished and the last notes died away, there was complete silence. And then the whole class (even Russell Ornelas) burst into clapping and cheering.

"That was cool," said Nancy Burgess—herself the coolest girl in the class. Matt sat down quietly. He had never felt so good in his life.

At the end of the school year, Matt's class had a graduation party in the auditorium. They had planned to sing their class theme song, and at the last minute, Nancy made a suggestion. "We could start as a group, and then let Matt take over and sing the last two verses as a solo." Matt agreed.

The parents, teachers, and students applauded warmly and called Matt out to take a special bow. "Thank y-you very m-much," Matt said.

"And thank *you*, Mrs. Johnson!" he added, clearly.

Think it Over/Write About It

1. What do you think Matt feared most about giving his oral report?
2. How did Matt overcome his fears?
3. What part did Mrs. Johnson play in helping Matt to overcome his fears? Did anyone else help?
4. Think about a time when you were afraid. How did you overcome your fears? Who helped you? How did they help?

Feeling Afraid

There is nothing wrong with feeling afraid. Fear is a natural instinct that helps people survive in the face of danger. The physical and emotional reactions that accompany fear can actually give people amazing strength and endurance. Mentally, fear can serve as a warning to be cautious and alert and not to take foolish chances.

But we are not only afraid of situations that threaten our survival. Fear comes in many forms, for many reasons. Sometimes, fear can *keep* us from the kind of action that leads to emotional and spiritual growth. It's important to face our fears, so that we can judge whether they are helping us or hurting us.

One kind of fear is the *fear of consequences*. This type of fear asks: What will happen if I do this? What will happen if I don't? What will this action cost me? These are good questions to ask, especially when our *conscience* tells us that a choice or action will have damaging consequences. But we need to be certain that the answers to these questions aren't clouded by unreasonable fears. In the story, Matt experienced the fear of consequences on both of these levels. He was afraid that his classmates would laugh if he stuttered in front of them. But he was also aware that if he did not give the oral report, he would fail his class.

Another kind of fear is the *fear of failure*. This fear can keep us from trying new things, meeting new people, or taking a chance on a new experience. In reasonable amounts, this kind of fear serves as a warning against taking unnecessary or dangerous risks. But many times, the simple fear of failure keeps people locked in a rut, blind to the possibilities that lie outside the everyday routine. Fear of failure, for example, might have kept Matt from the pleasure he got—and the pleasure he gave to others—by singing at the graduation party.

Gifts and Talents

At one time or another, everyone feels afraid. The Gospels tell us that even Jesus experienced fear. He was afraid that His disciples would lose faith and leave Him *(John 6:60–67)*. He feared dying on the cross *(Matthew 26:36–46)*. Yet Jesus never let His fears stand in the way of brave and loving action. He showed His followers that love can conquer fear.

To remind us that fear is sometimes crippling, Jesus told this *parable*:

A rich man who was going away called in his servants and entrusted his possessions to

them. To one servant, the man gave five talents (silver coins); to another, he gave two; and to the third, one—each according to his abilities. Then the man went away on a year's journey.

When the master returned, he called in his servants to settle their accounts. The first servant, who had received five talents, presented his master with these and with an additional five, which he had made by good investments. The second servant had doubled his two talents in the same way.

"Well done," the master smiled. "You will be rewarded."

Then, the third servant came forward. "Master," he said, "I knew that you were a demanding person. I was afraid I would lose your talent if I took chances with it. So, I buried it. Here it is, safe."

To the servant's surprise, the master was furious. "You wicked, lazy person!" he cried. "Couldn't you at least have put my money in a bank, where it would have earned some interest? Now, give your talent to the man who has ten, and get out of my sight!" *(Matthew 25:14–30).*

Jesus' listeners took this story to heart. They understood that it was more than financial advice. Like the master in the story, God

has given each of us certain "talents" and gifts. If we use them wisely—for our own good and the good of others—we will be rewarded. But if we allow the fear of failure to cripple us, we will never know the joy that wise use of our talents can bring.

■ ■ ■

Religious Vocabulary

Conscience The inner power that helps us tell right from wrong. Every Catholic has the duty to "inform" or develop his or her conscience through study of the Church's moral teachings and through prayer.

Parable A special kind of teaching story that gives us an insight into the way God wants us

to act. In His teaching, Jesus often used parables.

The gift of courage The gift of the Holy Spirit that helps us to act on our beliefs, to use our God-given talents bravely, and to reach out to others in loving service.

with the "false courage" that makes some people turn to drugs or drinking or violence to escape from or mask their fears. And the courage of the Holy Spirit is no magic trick that will make our talents blossom overnight.

Instead, the gift of courage is a special kind of strength rooted in love for God. The word "courage" itself comes from the Latin word for "heart"; with the Spirit's gift of courage, we "take heart," we are *encouraged*, even in times of fear and doubt. When we use the gift of courage, as Matt did in the story, we allow ourselves to receive help from others, knowing we don't have to go it alone. We look inward for the resources (the gifts and talents) God has entrusted to us, and we put them to good use.

In every age, Christians have performed truly heroic actions of love and service—some even risking their lives—by drawing on the Spirit's gift of courage. They did so knowing that their actions would bring about a better world, and would serve as a model of what God wants for each of us.

Your world is no less risky than theirs. The talents you have been given by God are no less needed.

Take Heart

The fears we face are very real to us. We can't overcome our fears, or put our talents to good use, without help. So, the Holy Spirit offers us the *gift of courage*.

The Spirit's gift of courage is not simply the absence of fear. It has nothing in common

Think It Over/Write About It

1. Give an example of how fear can serve as a positive warning. Give an example of how fear can keep us from doing what is right.
2. If Jesus were to ask you to give an accounting of how you have used your talents, what would you say? What would His response be?
3. Think of a situation facing young teens today that calls for a courageous response. Then, tell how the Holy Spirit's gift of courage would help you in facing this situation.

The Holy Spirit

In our world, there are many needs and problems. Some of them—such as world hunger, poverty, and the threat of nuclear war—can leave us feeling completely helpless. "What's the use?" our fears prompt us to ask. "What can one person possibly do to make a difference? What if we try our best—and we still fail?"

Jesus knew that His disciples, being human, asked themselves these same questions. So, on the night before He died, Jesus gave His friends both a great challenge and a wonderful promise. By washing their feet, like the lowliest Servant, Jesus challenged His friends to bring love and service to *all* people, everywhere *(John 13:5–15)*. And because He knew that they would be afraid of their own weakness and loneliness, Jesus promised them a Helper, a *Paraclete*, who would be with them always *(John 14:15–26)*.

The Helper whom Jesus promised is with us, too. When we pray, in the Apostles' Creed, "I believe in the Holy Spirit," we are proclaiming our belief in the Third Person of the Trinity. As the Father brings us life and the Son saves us from sin, so the Holy Spirit strengthens us for a life of holiness, service, and love.

With the words of the Creed, we are accepting the challenge as well as the promise of the Holy Spirit. We are saying that we will try to listen to the Spirit's call, rather than to the voice of our fears. We say that we will try to act with courage, and not give in to despair. We say that we will do our best to develop the talents and skills our world needs.

Breaking Out

Even with Jesus' promise alive in their hearts, the Apostles continued to experience fear and to doubt their own gifts. For a time, after Jesus returned to His Father, fear and doubt completely crippled the Apostles. They hid behind locked doors in the room where they had shared the Last Supper. They had been sent by Jesus to bring His Good News to the whole world, yet they were afraid to open a window!

But on the morning of *Pentecost*, Jesus' promise came true. Scripture tells us that the Apostles felt the presence of the Holy Spirit in a sudden and dramatic fashion. They heard a great wind, and saw tongues of fire appearing over their heads. But these were only outward symbols of the great change that had taken place inside them.

Filled with the Holy Spirit, and on fire with His gift of courage, the once-frightened Apostles burst from their hiding place. They went out into the streets and began to speak, clearly and movingly, of Jesus and His message. At first, their listeners were amazed. A few even laughed. But instead of arresting the Apostles—or, even worse, just walking away—the crowds began to hear and to believe. Thousands were baptized that day *(Acts of the Apostles 2:1–41)*.

Your Confirmation most probably won't be accompanied by dramatic outward signs of the Spirit's presence. But you will be renewed in that same Spirit, whom you received in Baptism. The same gift of courage will be stirred up in you. And you will be called to take the same Good News to *your* world, in the form of love and service.

The Courage to Serve

"I can't do it," Joan responded in prayer. "I'm too young. There has to be someone better than me."

"There is no one else in all of France," said the voices Joan heard in her heart. "If you want to keep the English from your land, and restore the crown prince to his rightful throne, you must act."

The young shepherd girl lowered her head. She was frightened. The whole country of France was frightened, ever since the English armies had invaded. For years, no French king had sat on the throne, and the French were prisoners in their own land. Even with all his advisors and generals, the heir to the throne could do nothing.

"Prince Charles will never go along with this plan!" Joan cried out, silently. "Why would he let me—a poor, uneducated girl—lead his armies? I don't know how to fight. I've never even ridden a horse!"

But the voices of Saint Catherine and Saint Margaret, who spoke to the young girl in prayer, were firm. "You will learn the skills you need. God will help you—and you will help your people."

Joan trembled with fear. But she knew the Spirit of truth was with her.

Convincing Prince Charles was even more difficult than Joan had imagined. But after a year of Joan's simple, honest advice, Prince Charles allowed himself to be crowned as king in defiance of the English orders. And Joan found herself leading the French armies into battle. The sight of this seemingly fearless young girl, dressed in white armor and carrying a banner with the names of Jesus and Mary, inspired the soldiers. Eventually, they drove the English armies out of France.

Joan of Arc, the patron saint of France, did not live to see the end of the battle. She was captured, tried, and executed by the English. She was only nineteen years old when she gave her life for her people and her faith.

Faith and Courage

Saint Joan of Arc was only a teenager when she faced the army that oppressed her nation. She feared failure and she feared being laughed at. But the need to act in love and service was greater than her fear, and so Joan was free to break out of the *apathy* that kept even kings and generals from acting.

What gave Saint Joan this freedom was her faith. Working with the Spirit's gift of courage, faith helps us act in the face of fear and difficulty. Another name for the gift of courage is *fortitude*, which means "the strength to go on even when things look hopeless."

When you look at the problems that face your world—gang violence, hunger and poverty, injustice of all kinds—you might be tempted to fall into apathy and inaction. The Holy Spirit's gift of courage or fortitude will

not make the problems go away. But working with faith, courage, hope, and your own skills and talents, you can make a difference.

Part of your preparation for Confirmation involves making a commitment to Christian service. This commitment is not meant to

■ ■ ■

Religious Vocabulary

Paraclete A scriptural term for the Holy Spirit; the word "Paraclete" is Greek for "one who speaks for or defends the rights of others."

Pentecost The Christian feast that celebrates the coming of the Holy Spirit to the Apostles. The Jews of Jesus' time celebrated a feast by the same name, commemorating the giving of the Ten Commandments to Moses. The word "Pentecost" means "fifty days"; the Spirit came to the Apostles fifty days after Jesus' Resurrection.

Apathy A word that means "lack of feeling." Apathy keeps people from acting in love and service, out of fear, hopelessness, or indifference to the needs of others.

Fortitude Another name for the Holy Spirit's gift of courage. "Fortitude" means "the strength to endure."

be a way of earning the gifts of the Holy Spirit, which are already yours through Baptism. Instead, practicing Christian service now helps you sharpen your skills and talents for a lifetime of serving others in love, in Jesus' name.

Volunteering in a soup kitchen, tutoring a young child, visiting an elderly person, or cleaning up a littered neighborhood park may seem like very small actions. But even these require courage: the courage to believe that you have something to give, the courage to act when others say it's not cool, or even useless. Through the actions of Christians all through the centuries—whether raising the banner of freedom for a nation, or washing the feet of one poor homeless person—God's kingdom of justice and peace is built. Each time you dare to make a difference, the light of hope, like the flame of the Holy Spirit, is a little easier to see.

Think It Over/Write About It

1. What do you mean when you say, "I believe in the Holy Spirit"?
2. How did the Holy Spirit's gift of courage make a difference in the Apostles' lives? In Saint Joan's life?
3. What are some ways you can begin, right now, to practice using your gifts and talents in service to others?
4. Think about situations that make you feel hopeless or powerless. How does the Spirit's gift of courage or fortitude help you face these situations?

The Gift of Courage

Put yourself in each of the following situations. For each example, briefly answer these two questions: (A) What am I afraid of? (B) How can I respond to this situation with courage?

1. Your math test is tomorrow. You can't really study because you don't understand the problems.

   (A) _____

   (B) _____

2. You are walking alone on a nearly-empty street. Ahead of you, a shabbily dressed man staggers and then falls to the curb.

   (A) _____

   (B) _____

3. You live with your grandmother. Yesterday, she got very sick and had to go to the hospital.

   (A) _____

   (B) _____

4. Today is the first day of gym class. Your mother bought you the wrong kind of shoes because they were on sale and the family budget is tight.

   (A) _____

   (B) _____

5. Someone has been selling drugs to the children at the elementary school. On your way past the schoolyard, you see some kids gathered around a parked car. You think you recognize the car.

   (A) _____

   (B) _____

True or False

Circle the T if the statement is true. Circle the F if the statement is false.

1. Fear is only a problem for babies and weaklings.   T   F

2. There are times when being afraid can serve as a positive warning.   T   F

3. The Holy Spirit's gift of courage helps you use your own skills and talents to help others.   T   F

4. If you are really afraid, it is OK to use drugs or violence to cover up your fears.   T   F

5. Faith works with the gift of courage to give you the strength to act even when things look hopeless.   T   F

6. You can only receive the gifts of the Holy Spirit after you have put in many hours of Christian service.   T   F

7. The story of Saint Joan of Arc shows that young people really cannot make any difference in the world.   T   F

8. Fortitude is another name for the Holy Spirit's gift of courage.   T   F

9. At the Last Supper, Jesus gave His Apostles the challenge to serve all people, but He did not give them any help.   T   F

10. The Holy Spirit is the Third Person of the Trinity.   T   F

Vocabulary Review

Look up each of the following words in the Glossary which begins on page 117. Then, write a short paragraph that uses each word correctly.

courage	Holy Spirit	service
fortitude	Pentecost	talent

_____

_____

_____

_____

_____

_____

Christian Service

As part of your preparation for Confirmation, you may be required to participate in a Christian service project. This is not a "payment" you make in order to be confirmed; participation in Christian service is a way to practice using your skills and talents to help others. Because being an adult Catholic means loving and serving others throughout your life, it is a good idea to begin participating in a Christian service project now, whether or not it is a requirement of your Confirmation program.

It is important that your choice of a Christian service project be something *specific* and practical that you can do for others; that it involve using your skills and talents to meet a real need in your parish or neighborhood; and that it is something you give time and effort to outside your everyday responsibilities. You can work alone or in a group.

Here are some points to think about when planning your service project. Discuss your plans with your family, your sponsor, your teacher, and your classmates.

- Think about people's needs, problems, and fears. Ask yourself what you can do to help. Who needs time, effort, service, and love from you? What do you have to share?
- Make specific plans ahead of time. If you will be working within an established program (like a soup kitchen or a convalescent home), get the necessary permissions and make arrangements with a supervisor.
- Carry out your project on a regular basis, within an agreed-upon time frame. (Don't just dash in and out of one hospital room, one afternoon.) Keep your agreements with group members and with those you serve; be there when you say you will be.
- Throughout your project, take time to think and pray about your actions. You may want to keep a journal of your experiences. Each day, put the success of your project in God's hands, and ask the Holy Spirit's help in overcoming your fears.
- When your project is completed, look back over your experience. Make plans to follow up on what you have begun. Investigate other ways you can continue to be of service, to your parish and your community, after your Confirmation.

Reverence and Courage

These two gifts of the Holy Spirit may seem quite different, but in reality they complement each other. Use the outline on this page to help you pray for the ability to serve God and others with love. You can pray by yourself, with your classmates, or with your family.

Scripture Readings (Choose 1 or 2):
    Psalm 121 (Take courage in the Lord)
    Psalm 145:1–10 (All that we do honors the Lord)
    Luke 10:25–28 (Love of God and neighbor)
    Romans 8:31–39 (The love of Christ gives us hope and power)

Music: Choose a hymn, song, or piece of instrumental music that has meaning for you—one that speaks to the theme of your prayer. Sing or listen to the music.

Sharing Experience: Think about a time when you have experienced the value of the talents and skills God has given you. If you are praying with others, share your experience.

Prayer: Read the following prayer of petition aloud. If you are praying with others, form two groups to read alternate lines.
    Lord, we are afraid:
        Send Your Spirit to comfort and guide us.
    Lord, we are too young:
        Speak in our hearts, and tell us that now is our time to act.
    Lord, too many people around us are hungry and hurting:
        Help us believe that we can make a difference.
    Lord, it looks hopeless!
        Show us Your face. Fill us with the fire of hope!

Close by praying this prayer of Saint Ignatius Loyola:

Teach us, good Lord, to serve You as You deserve: to give and not count the cost; to fight and not heed the wounds; to toil and not seek to rest; to labor and not ask for any reward but the knowledge that we do Your will, through Christ Jesus our Lord.

5

Community of Believers

In This Chapter

- You will think about what it means to understand others and to be understood yourself.
- You will learn that the Holy Spirit's gift of understanding helps you to make sense of your faith and to relate to others with patience and compassion.
- You will see that understanding is a real part of the Church, the community of faith.

The Challenge

- To see that real relationships depend on understanding as well as knowledge
- To know that God understands me, and wants me to understand Him, myself, and others
- To find my place in the Catholic Church, the community of believers

One on One

Danielle and her father weren't talking. It had been that way for the whole long ride from their house to the church parking lot. Now, as they sat in silence in the hot parked car, Danielle felt as though she were in the stuffy waiting room of the dentist's office.

The tension had started earlier that morning, when Danielle's teacher, Mrs. Diaz, had called. She said that she needed to "interview" Danielle to understand more about Danielle's attitude toward her upcoming Confirmation. Danielle agreed to meet Mrs. Diaz by the benches in the church lot.'

As Danielle was on her way out the door to the bus stop, her father stopped her. "Come on," he offered. "Let me give you a lift."

Danielle was feeling cranky, though she wasn't sure why. Maybe it was the idea of the

interview—it felt like a test. She was hoping to take a few minutes, alone on the bus, to sort out her thoughts. But here was her dad, grinning cheerfully, breaking in on her bad mood.

"Oh, all right," Danielle sighed, not at all grateful.

Mrs. Diaz was late for their appointment. "What do you think she'll ask you?" Danielle's father spoke up, trying to break the silence.

"I have no idea," Danielle snapped.

And they sat, silent again, until Mrs. Diaz arrived.

"Let's sit outside, on the bench," Mrs. Diaz suggested. She smiled at Danielle's father. "Mr. Ross, you're welcome to join us."

Danielle shot her father the same icy look she always gave him when he sang too loud in church. Mr. Ross got the point.

"I think I'll wait in the car," he said. "There's a ball game on the radio."

Danielle sat at the picnic table across from her teacher. She liked Mrs. Diaz well enough. At least Mrs. Diaz didn't lecture all the time; she let the kids in the Confirmation class talk about their ideas. But Danielle wasn't crazy about this interview. It wasn't easy going "one on one" with an adult—especially with her father watching from the car.

Mrs. Diaz began by explaining the purpose of the interview. She and the other teachers and members of the parish staff were interested in what prompted the students to join the Confirmation program.

"Why do you want to be confirmed?" Mrs. Diaz asked Danielle.

This was the kind of question Danielle was prepared for. "My whole family is Catholic," she answered. "I want to be Catholic, too." Then, seeing that Mrs. Diaz was obviously expecting more, Danielle added, "And I want to learn about Jesus and about my religion."

Mrs. Diaz smiled, but seemed unimpressed. "What kind of Catholic do want to be, Danielle?" she asked.

Danielle thought for a minute. "The good kind," she said, finally. "You know, a person who goes to Mass and . . . uh, sends my children to religion class."

Mrs. Diaz had one more question. "What talents or gifts do you have to share with the parish community?"

"I'm not sure," Danielle shrugged. "I like to sing. Maybe I could be in the choir or something."

Mrs. Diaz thanked Danielle and gathered up her notes. This interview had been very much like all the others: short answers to serious questions. Mrs. Diaz had hoped for something more, but she wasn't sure how to ask for it.

Back at the car, Danielle saw her mother, chatting with her dad as she rocked two tiny babies in their twin carriage. Danielle bent down to hug the babies, grinning.

"Hi, you guys!" she said. "What're you doing here?" Both babies chirped and clapped at Danielle, happily.

"We were just out for our walk," Mrs. Ross said. "How did your interview go?"

"OK, I guess," Danielle said. "Can I walk the twins back home?"

She headed off, pushing the double carriage and singing. Mrs. Diaz joined Danielle's parents at the car.

"I didn't know Danielle had a brother and sister," Mrs. Diaz said, after greeting the Rosses.

"You mean she didn't tell you?" Mrs. Ross asked, in surprise. "They're our foster children—and they're just about the most important people in Danielle's life right now.

"The twins were born addicted to narcotics," Mrs. Ross continued. "Their mother was an addict. Danielle helps me with those babies day and night. I don't think she's had more than four hours of sleep a night since they came to us."

Mr. Ross nodded. "She holds those babies and rocks them when they cry. She helps her mom feed them. She changes their diapers. And she still squeezes in time for her schoolwork. I can't believe she didn't mention them to you!"

As Mrs. Diaz watched Danielle walk away, she smiled. Then, she tore up the notes she had made during Danielle's interview. What she had learned from Danielle's parents helped her understand far more than any answers on a printed form.

Think It Over/Write About It

1. What was Danielle expecting from the interview? Why was she so irritable toward her father?
2. Besides singing, what other gifts and talents does Danielle have to share?
3. What was Mrs. Diaz expecting from the interview? Why did she tear up her notes?
4. If someone were to ask you why you want to be confirmed, what would your answer be? What would help someone understand you and your answer better?

More Than Knowing

As Mrs. Diaz learned, it takes more than one quick interview to really understand another person. By the time she tore up her notes, the teacher had learned some very important things about Danielle. By watching the way Danielle acted with the babies, and by listening to what Danielle's parents said about her. Mrs. Diaz was able to "read between the lines" of the girl's simple answers. More than just knowing her student, Mrs. Diaz came to understand Danielle.

Real understanding is a rare quality. We may know a lot about our best friends; we may have shared information about ourselves with them that no one else knows. Yet there are times when even best friends don't understand each other.

It's the same with parents and children, who know one another best, but may not always understand. Danielle's father knew she had been up late helping with the babies, but at first he didn't understand why his daughter was so cranky. Danielle knew that her father loved her and was anxious to support her in the interview, but she didn't understand why he wouldn't just leave her alone.

We don't always understand ourselves, either. Danielle wasn't sure what had caused her bad mood. She did not understand herself well enough to recognize the gifts she had to offer.

Putting It All Together

"To understand" literally means "to know what stands under something," to grasp the truth or meaning that may be partly hidden in a person or a situation. In order to reach understanding, it is sometimes necessary to "stand outside" our own experience and see the situation from another point of view. Just as an instant-replay camera helps sports officials make a difficult call, by showing a play from many angles, so understanding helps us see the world—and ourselves—through others' eyes.

Every one of our relationships—with ourselves, our families, our friends, our teachers—depends on understanding. It is a skill we can practice by being open and honest and avoiding words or actions that will be easily misunderstood. We can also look for understanding from others. A sign of a good relationship, one that is built on real love and honesty, is that people take time to try to understand one another.

Sometimes, understanding comes in a flash, like getting the answer to a math problem without really thinking about it. We say, "Aha! I see it now!" More commonly, we grow

into understanding in a slow process, like assembling a complicated jigsaw puzzle. Over time, what looked like a confused mass of shapes and colors comes together, and we "get the picture." And sometimes, we just aren't able to understand at all. We have to trust in the word and the help of someone who *does* understand. One Person in whom we can put our trust is the Holy Spirit.

The Spirit of Understanding

God, who understands us so completely, knows that we sometimes have a difficult time understanding Him. But God *wants* us to draw closer to Him, to enter into a real, loving relationship with Him and with His Creation. And so, God sends us His Spirit of understanding.

The *gift of understanding* helps us make sense out of what we know and believe about God, about Jesus Christ, about the Church. It helps us "get the point" of the Scripture readings we hear at Mass—sometimes in a flash, sometimes over a long period of time. The Spirit's gift of understanding does not always give us all the answers about our faith, because there will always be *mysteries*. But the gift of understanding can help us ask good, thoughtful questions.

Just as the Holy Spirit's gift of understanding helps strengthen our relationship with God, so it helps deepen our relationships with others. With understanding, we begin to see our lives from another point of view: God's point of view. We come to see our relationships with parents, teachers, and friends as part of God's wonderful plan for us. The gift of understanding also helps us admit that we do not know everything, and that we still have a lot to learn about ourselves and about life.

■ ■ ■

Religious Vocabulary

The gift of understanding The gift of the Holy Spirit that helps us see the truth in our relationship with God, with others, and with ourselves.

Mission A God-given task or duty in life. The mission of Jesus was to bring the Good News of God's saving love.

Mystery An article of faith (such as the existence of the Trinity, or the fact of Jesus' Resurrection) that we believe, even though we do not fully understand it.

Jesus and Understanding

An important part of Jesus' *mission* was to help people grow in the gift of understanding. By the way He treated others, Jesus showed that He truly understood their needs and their hopes. Through the stories He told, Jesus helped His listeners understand more about themselves, about one another, and about God.

And when He Himself faced the worst kind of human fear and doubt, Jesus gave us

an example of how we are to act when we do not understand. Kneeling in the garden, moments before His arrest, Jesus prayed, "Father, if it is possible, let this cup pass from Me; yet, not as I will, but as You will" (*Matthew 26:39*). In total trust, which is the gift of understanding taken to its farthest limit, Jesus put His life in the hands of His Father.

Jesus left us some very practical advice about using the gift of understanding:

1. Treat others as you want them to treat you (*Matthew 7:12*).
2. Strive for peace with everyone (*Matthew 5:21–26*).
3. Reach out in love to others, even your enemies (*Matthew 5:43–48*).
4. Put God first in your life and in your search for understanding, and everything else will follow (*Matthew 6:33*).

If you put this advice about understanding into practice, you will be able to recognize God more clearly in people who are poor, and in people who serve the poor. You will be more likely to see God in people who forgive, and in people who ask for forgiveness. The gift of understanding brings the written words of the Good News to life in the people that we meet.

Think It Over/Write About It

1. Who understands you best? How do you know?
2. What kinds of problems are caused by a lack of understanding?
3. How can the Holy Spirit's gift of understanding help you in your relationship with yourself? With your family and friends? With people you do not know? With God?
4. Think of one area of your faith you would like to understand better. Write a prayer asking God's help. You might want to phrase your prayer as a short list of questions.

Belonging to the Church

In order to grow in understanding, it helps to feel that we ourselves are understood: that we fit in somewhere, that someone cares enough about us to help us make sense of things.

Our community of faith, the Catholic Church, is one important place where we seek understanding. The people who form this community can help us learn about God and about how to make sense out of our own lives. Our fellow Catholics can help us with our questions because *every* member of the Church—from the person in the pew next to you at Mass to the pope himself—is involved in the same search for faith and meaning.

We call the Church (which was born in the Spirit-filled events of Pentecost) by many names: People of God, Community of Believers, Body of Christ. All of these titles mean that we are bound together in some way. One of these bonds is a common understanding of the basic teachings of Jesus which we find in the Bible and in the *tradition* of the Church. Another bond is structural: we share a common loyalty and obedience to the leadership of the pope and the bishops, the successors of the Apostles. And still another bond is our common mission as members of the Church: to share with others our understandings of God's Word and the Way of Jesus.

Communion of Saints

In the Apostle's Creed, we pray, "I believe in . . . the holy catholic church, the communion of saints. . . ." This statement of belief gives us more ways to look at the Church, more ways to understand how we belong.

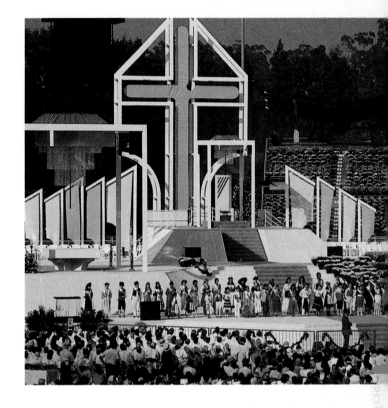

The word *Church* itself comes from a Greek word that means "belonging to God." When we call ourselves Church, we are saying we understand that we belong to God.

When we call ourselves "catholic," in the Apostles' Creed, we are going back to the earliest Greek use of this word, which means "universal, for everyone." (This use of the word is not limited to Roman Catholic Christians like us; many other Christian denominations pray the Creed in the same words.) By the title *Catholic*, we are saying that we understand that no one is left out of our relationship with God. All people, if they truly want to know and follow Jesus, are welcome in our community.

Describing ourselves as universal also reminds us that the Church we belong to is much bigger than the congregation gathered in our parish church. Our common understanding joins us with every other Catholic, all around the world.

The man's musical accent reminded Martin of his mother's voice. She had been a black woman, herself the child of slaves.

"God cares," Martin answered quietly. "And I care, too."

Martin cleaned the slaves' open sores, and gave them healthy food to eat. He listened to their fears and worries. He tried to comfort them.

When he had done all he could, Martin headed back to Casa Rosario, the Dominican priory in Lima where he lived. There would be another slave ship soon enough, he knew.

In the crowded city street, a poor Indian woman approached him. "Brother Martin," she gasped, handing him her baby, "you helped me last year when I was sick. Take my baby, please. I have no money to feed her."

We are even united with the those who are no longer living. When we call ourselves the *communion of saints*, we are saying that our faith family is not broken up by death. All those believers who have gone before us are part of our Church. Some of these men and women are especially remembered for the way they lived out their mission to follow Jesus. We honor them in prayer as *canonized* saints.

Saint Martin's Mission

Another slave ship had entered the port of Callao, just outside Lima, Peru. Martin de Porres waited until it had docked. Then, he boarded the ship with his box of medicines, and began to bandage the wounds of the slaves he found shivering below the decks.

"Why are you doing this?" one black man asked Martin. "Nobody cares about us."

Before Martin could protest, the woman disappeared. Martin looked down at the crying baby. In that small and helpless face, Martin could see his own childhood, and the father who had abandoned him.

"Ah, *pobrecita*, poor little one," Martin sighed. "I understand why you cry."

Martin took the baby to his sister, who agreed to take care of the little one. Soon, other people began bringing their children to Brother Martin—children they were too poor to feed or clothe.

Eventually, Martin founded an orphanage for the abandoned children of Lima. He started a free clinic for people who could not pay for care when they were sick or injured. He gave out blankets and food to the hungry, visited prisoners in jail, and continued his work with the slaves. Brother Martin even took in stray dogs and cats that he found on the streets.

"We are all God's children," Martin would explain. "Whenever one suffers, the others suffer, too. We are one in our sorrows and in our joys."

Understanding and Faith

Saint Martin de Porres, who is the patron of social justice, understood the poor and the outcast of Lima. Martin had been poor and

■ ■ ■

Religious Vocabulary

Tradition The beliefs passed along from generation to generation by the Church; all Church teaching is based on Scripture and tradition.

Catholic Church The most common name for our community of faith; the worldwide community of Christians who follow the pope and the bishops. Also called Roman Catholic Church, because the traditional home diocese of the pope, the first among bishops, is Rome.

Communion of saints All members of the Church, living and dead, who are united in their common faith in Jesus.

Canonization The formal process by which the Church declares that a person has lived an outstanding Christian life and is worthy of being honored and imitated. One who has been canonized receives the title of "Saint"; his or her life is celebrated on a particular feast day.

Grace A share in God's own life; friendship with God.

outcast himself, and he saw all people as his brothers and sisters in Christ.

Faith worked with the Holy Spirit's gift of understanding to help Martin see how he could best live his life as a Christian. It can do the same thing for us.

You are not canonized, like Martin de Porres—but you *are* a saint. The word "saint" means "holy one." Holiness is the quality of being filled with *grace*, of encouraging God's life to grow and increase within you. By your membership in the Church through Baptism, you share in the Church's own holiness. You will continue to grow in holiness through Confirmation.

You can use faith and the support of the Church community to search for the very best way *you* can live a Christian life. You can begin where Saint Martin began, with the people you meet and spend time with every day—your family and your friends, your teachers and classmates. Continue to ask questions. Continue to put yourself in the place of others, so that you can begin to put the pieces together and grow in understanding and holiness.

Your mission as a Catholic Christian does not end with Confirmation. Your life as a saint is just beginning.

Think It Over/Write About It

1. How can belonging to the Church help you grow in understanding?
2. Name three things that members of the Church have in common.
3. Why is it important to ask questions about your faith?
4. How would you define a saint? Can you see yourself in your definition? How can you grow in holiness right now, right where you are?

Understanding Others

An important part of understanding is putting yourself in another person's position—seeing things from another point of view. This attitude helps build community in the parish; it is expressed in the sign of peace at Mass.

Think about how the gift of understanding can help you reach out to each of the people listed below. For each person, write on practical way you could show a spirit of understanding in your attitudes or actions.

1. Someone who is homeless

   _____

2. Someone who has authority over you

   _____

3. Someone of a difference race than you

   _____

4. Someone who dislikes you

   _____

5. Someone who is physically disabled

   _____

6. Someone you have hurt

   _____

7. Someone who is always asking for your help

   _____

8. Someone from a rival school

   _____

9. Someone who is younger than you

   _____

10. Someone who is elderly

   _____

Being Catholic

Put a check next to the definition below that comes closest to your own understanding of the Church.

_____ 1. The Church is the People of God.

_____ 2. The Church is the place where God is worshiped.

_____ 3. The Church is the pope, bishops, and priests.

_____ 4. The Church is a group of people who share the same beliefs.

_____ 5. The Church is a nonprofit organization that performs charitable work.

Rewrite the definition you chose, adding whatever you need to explain what the Church means to you.

_____

_____

At this time in your life, how do you feel about being a Catholic?

_____

_____

Vocabulary Review

Look up each of the following terms in the Glossary which begins on page 117. (Some of these words may be new to you, but they all have to do with the Church.) Then, choose four words or phrases and use them in complete sentences.

bishop	deacon	parish
Catholic Church	diocese	pastor
communion of saints	encyclical letter	priest

1. _____

_____

2. _____

_____

3. _____

_____

4. _____

_____

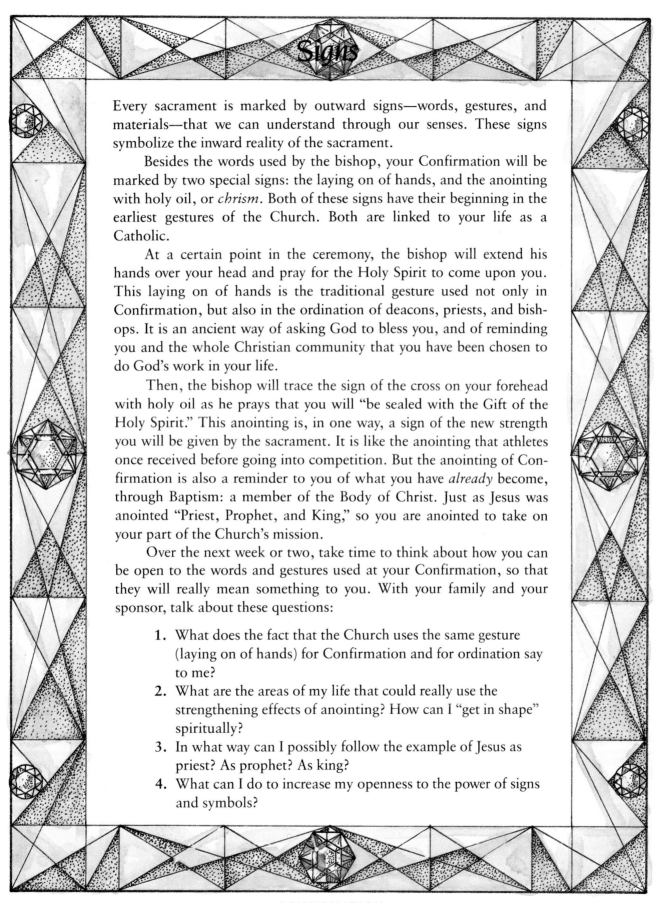

Signs

Every sacrament is marked by outward signs—words, gestures, and materials—that we can understand through our senses. These signs symbolize the inward reality of the sacrament.

Besides the words used by the bishop, your Confirmation will be marked by two special signs: the laying on of hands, and the anointing with holy oil, or *chrism*. Both of these signs have their beginning in the earliest gestures of the Church. Both are linked to your life as a Catholic.

At a certain point in the ceremony, the bishop will extend his hands over your head and pray for the Holy Spirit to come upon you. This laying on of hands is the traditional gesture used not only in Confirmation, but also in the ordination of deacons, priests, and bishops. It is an ancient way of asking God to bless you, and of reminding you and the whole Christian community that you have been chosen to do God's work in your life.

Then, the bishop will trace the sign of the cross on your forehead with holy oil as he prays that you will "be sealed with the Gift of the Holy Spirit." This anointing is, in one way, a sign of the new strength you will be given by the sacrament. It is like the anointing that athletes once received before going into competition. But the anointing of Confirmation is also a reminder to you of what you have *already* become, through Baptism: a member of the Body of Christ. Just as Jesus was anointed "Priest, Prophet, and King," so you are anointed to take on your part of the Church's mission.

Over the next week or two, take time to think about how you can be open to the words and gestures used at your Confirmation, so that they will really mean something to you. With your family and your sponsor, talk about these questions:

1. What does the fact that the Church uses the same gesture (laying on of hands) for Confirmation and for ordination say to me?
2. What are the areas of my life that could really use the strengthening effects of anointing? How can I "get in shape" spiritually?
3. In what way can I possibly follow the example of Jesus as priest? As prophet? As king?
4. What can I do to increase my openness to the power of signs and symbols?

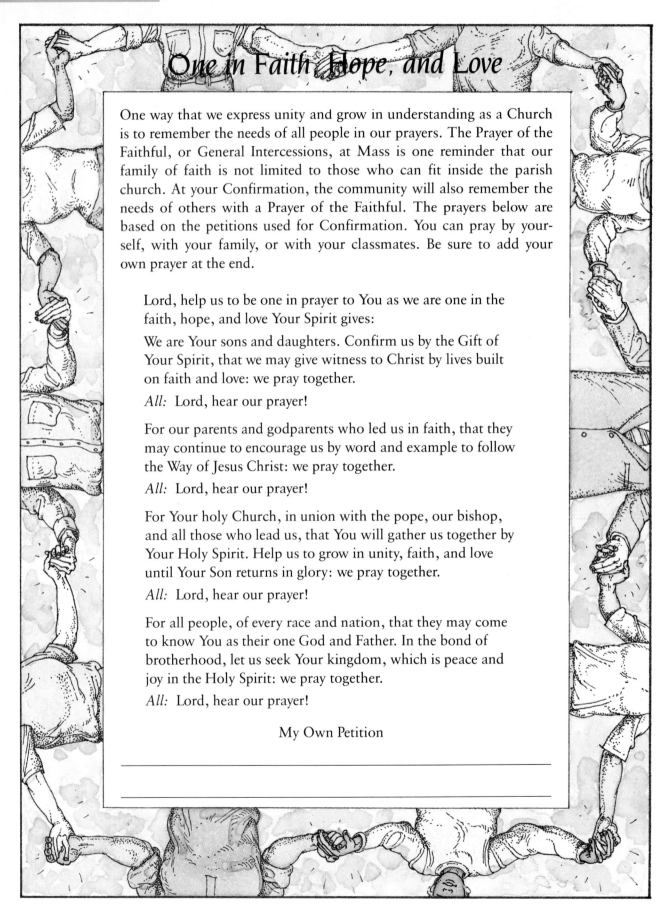

One in Faith, Hope, and Love

One way that we express unity and grow in understanding as a Church is to remember the needs of all people in our prayers. The Prayer of the Faithful, or General Intercessions, at Mass is one reminder that our family of faith is not limited to those who can fit inside the parish church. At your Confirmation, the community will also remember the needs of others with a Prayer of the Faithful. The prayers below are based on the petitions used for Confirmation. You can pray by yourself, with your family, or with your classmates. Be sure to add your own prayer at the end.

Lord, help us to be one in prayer to You as we are one in the faith, hope, and love Your Spirit gives:

We are Your sons and daughters. Confirm us by the Gift of Your Spirit, that we may give witness to Christ by lives built on faith and love: we pray together.

All: Lord, hear our prayer!

For our parents and godparents who led us in faith, that they may continue to encourage us by word and example to follow the Way of Jesus Christ: we pray together.

All: Lord, hear our prayer!

For Your holy Church, in union with the pope, our bishop, and all those who lead us, that You will gather us together by Your Holy Spirit. Help us to grow in unity, faith, and love until Your Son returns in glory: we pray together.

All: Lord, hear our prayer!

For all people, of every race and nation, that they may come to know You as their one God and Father. In the bond of brotherhood, let us seek Your kingdom, which is peace and joy in the Holy Spirit: we pray together.

All: Lord, hear our prayer!

My Own Petition

_____

_____

6

Covenant People

In This Chapter

- You will explore the role of decision-making in your own life.
- You will learn that right judgment, a gift of the Holy Spirit, can help you make good decisions.
- You will see that Catholics try to base their actions and choice on a covenant relationship with God.

The Challenge

- To see that it's possible for me to make good decisions.
- To take responsibility for my own moral growth, and to ask for God's help
- To see Confirmation as a time when I begin to live the promises others made for me in Baptism

Ballroom Manners

"OK, I give up," Marci grinned, shaking her head. "What *is* this 'Cotillion' thing, anyway?"

Mrs. Abrams, Marci's teacher at the new school, gathered up her books. "So, you've been hearing about our end-of-the-year tradition?" she smiled.

"It's all anybody talks about—especially the girls," said Marci. "But what's the big deal about a dance?"

"The Cotillion is more than a dance," Mrs. Abrams explained. "If you want to attend, you have to participate in the ballroom dancing class after school. You have to learn proper etiquette. And," Mrs. Abrams paused before she added the final requirement, "you have to bring your parents."

Marci thought about the Cotillion all through the next week. At her old school, the kids would have laughed at the idea of a formal party with parents invited. But here at Jefferson Intermediate, people talked about the Cotillion as if it were the best thing to happen at school since the gym flooded and P.E. classes were cancelled!

Marci wanted to fit. Somehow, she'd avoided the typical "new kid" problems, blending in right away with a nice group of friends. She wasn't going to do anything to call attention to herself now. So, Marci signed up for the ballroom dancing class.

Ballroom dancing *did* have its advantages, Marci learned. Everyone looked equally dumb for the first few weeks, trying to master the patterns of the dances. There was lots of good-natured laughter. And it wasn't all waltzes and two-steps. At the end of each class, the teacher let them listen to their favorite kinds of music and dance any way they wanted.

Etiquette class wasn't quite as much fun. It was hard to get excited about reviewing mealtime manners, learning to ask for a dance or accept an invitation, and practicing the business of introducing parents to teachers in a receiving line.

About a month before the Cotillion, the whole parent question came up in a new way. Tiffany and Gina, Marci's new best friends, suddenly decided it would be a great idea if their parents didn't show up for the dance. "I mean, who wants your mom and dad watching you dance?" complained Gina. "It would be *so* embarrassing!"

The two girls planned to tell their parents that attendance at the dance was "optional." They'd convince their parents that no other parents were bothering to go. Then, they'd tell Mrs. Abrams that their parents weren't able to attend because of illness or business trips.

"Come on, Marci," Tiffany coaxed. "You try it, too. You don't want *your* parents there, do you?"

Marci was confused. It might be fun to be at the dance on her own, but she knew her father was looking forward to it. The pressure to go along with her friends got even stronger when their plan actually worked: Mrs. Abrams gave Gina and Tiffany permission to attend the Cotillion without their parents.

"You want Mommy and Daddy watching if *David* asks you to dance?" Gina teased.

Marci made up her mind . . . sort of. The day before the Cotillion, she waited in her room. She planned to talk her parents out of attending the Cotillion at dinner that night. Then, she saw her dad get out of the car, carrying his good suit in a dry-cleaners' bag. One look at his face, and Marci knew she didn't have the heart to hurt his feelings.

The school auditorium was transformed for the Cotillion. Looking around while she

waited with her parents in the receiving line, Marci couldn't believe it. The scarred lunch tables were covered with crisp linen and decorated with floral centerpieces. Soft lights made the room look inviting. The students looked great with suits and dresses replacing their usual jeans and sweatshirts.

"Mom and Dad, I would like you to meet my teacher, Mrs. Abrams," Marci said, thankful for all the practice. "Mrs. Abrams, my parents—Mr. and Mrs. D'Amato." The formal manners were like the rest of the evening: kind of old-fashioned, Marci thought, but sweet, too.

After Marci and her parents had found the table with their placecards, Marci was surprised to see Gina and Tiffany. Gina called Marci aside.

"Can we sit with you and your folks?" Gina whispered, frantically.

"It feels so weird," added Tiffany. "Everybody's looking at us!"

Mr. D'Amato had already pulled over two extra chairs.

The three girls danced often. David even asked Marci to waltz, and all the parents applauded their children's ballroom dancing skills. Finally, the D.J. switched to some popular records.

"This one's a father-daughter dance," he announced, putting on a loud fast song.

Mr. D'Amato hung his suit coat carefully over the back of his chair. Then, he hesitated, looking at Marci. She smiled and held out her hand, and they headed for the dance floor.

Think It Over/Write About It

1. What were the requirements for attending the Cotillion? Do you think that fulfilling requirements and learning rules adds anything to an experience? Why or why not?
2. What things did Marci have to consider in making her decision? Why do you think she decided as she did?
3. How do you think Gina and Tiffany felt as they watched Marci dance with her father?
4. Think of a time when you made a difficult decision. Write about what went into your choice, and what the results were.

Making Good Decisions

In the story, Marci made several decisions. Each time, she had to consider a number of options. She had to choose between her initial resistance to the idea of the Cotillion and her need to fit in at the new school. She had to choose between having lots of free time and staying after school for the dance class. Finally, Marci had to choose between her friends' idea of what was cool and her father's feelings. Overall, Marci's decisions were good ones. She had reason to feel good about herself at the Cotillion.

Making good decisions (choices we can live with and feel good about) requires that we take several careful steps. Marci followed this reasoning process, although she wasn't always aware she was doing it. You can practice these steps so that they begin to come naturally.

First, you should understand the whole situation. What are your choices?

Second, you should consider the consequences of your decision. What will happen? How will other people be affected by your choice?

Finally, consider how you will feel about yourself and about the situation after you've made your decision. Keep a clear picture of the kind of person you want to be. How will your decision affect the way you think of yourself? Can you live comfortably with your choice?

Help!

We all face decisions every day—more and more decisions, the older we get. Some choices don't seem terribly important at the time. Others seem to carry so much weight that we're frightened of making the wrong move.

It's good to know that, in addition to the kind of reasoning process we go through when we make choices, there are some outside sources of help. Rules and customs are one very important aid to decision-making. Knowing what's expected of us in a particular situation can make it easier to choose the right course of action. Like Marci in her etiquette class, we might resist learning the rules at first, because we want to be independent; but like Marci in the reception line, we often discover that rules are reassuring!

Good advice is another important help. Unfortunately, the advice Marci got from her friends—to lie to parents and teachers in order to look "cool"—wasn't good. Fortunately, Marci trusted herself well enough to make the right choice.

Kinds of Decisions

Of course, not every decision we're faced with is as simple as choosing the right utensil to use at dinner, or even whether or not to include parents in a school activity. *Moral decisions*—which involve choosing between something which contributes to our own and others' spiritual growth, and something which might be harmful or even seriously sinful—are also a very real part of our lives. Drugs and alcohol, sexuality, the use of money and resources, relationships with family members and friends: all of these areas present young teens with the need to make good moral decisions.

We need to develop our moral decision-making skills, which include all those listed above. In the case of moral decisions, the reasoning process also includes prayer and reflection. Learning the rules includes forming our conscience through study of the Ten Commandments, the Beatitudes, and the laws of the Church. Getting good advice includes turning to parents, teachers, sponsors, and the parish priest for help, as well as turning to the Word of God in Scripture.

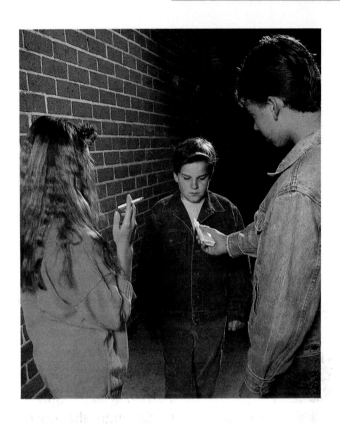

The Gift of Right Judgment

We can also turn to the Holy Spirit's gift of *right judgment*—the gift that helps us build on all the skills we have for making good moral choices. Like the other gifts of the

= = =

Religious Vocabulary

Moral decisions Choices that involve our Christian morality or sense of what is right (good for our relationship with God and with others) and wrong (sinful).

The gift of right judgment The gift of the Holy Spirit that helps us make good decisions and act on our beliefs.

Peer pressure Pressure from people your age to go along with the crowd or to fit in. Peer pressure can be positive or negative,

depending on whether the action you're being pressured into is right or wrong.

Intuition An inner sense of how to act. Intuition is rooted in thought and reasoning, but it seems to move faster.

Counsel Another name for the gift of right judgment. This name reminds us that right judgment includes asking others for help, and offering good advice and examples.

dance, the gift of right judgment gave her insight into her father's feelings. It helped Marci overcome the negative *peer pressure* she was experiencing from her friends.

Sometimes, the gift of right judgment works so quietly within us that it appears we haven't really had to work at a decision. We seem to be acting purely on *intuition*, without conscious thought. But the gift of right judgment helps bring thought and emotion, logic and intuition together. We use the Spirit's gift of right judgment best when we have prepared ourselves for good decision-making by prayer, study, and reasoning.

Good Counsel

Another name for the Spirit's gift of right judgment is *counsel*—the root word of "counselor," or someone who gives good advice. This name is a reminder to use of how we are to use this gift of the Spirit. We aren't meant to go it alone in life, facing tough choices without help. Instead, the Holy Spirit reminds us to seek good counsel from those we trust—and to *give* good counsel, advice, and example to others.

Spirit, right judgment is a way of looking at things—looking beyond the confusion and the outside pressures, to find the simplest, best decision.

The gift of right judgment gives us insight into ourselves, others, and situations. When Marci was trying to decide whether to discourage her parents from attending the

Think It Over/Write About It

1. What questions can you ask yourself to help you make a good decision? Where can you go for help?
2. How does the Holy Spirit's gift of right judgment affect the decision-making process? What does intuition have to do with it?
3. Why do you think it is important to give good advice as well as to ask for it?
4. What do you consider the most serious moral problem facing young people today? What messages do you hear from society or from your peers regarding this problem? How might you call on the Holy Spirit's gift of right judgment to help you decide on your response to this problem?

Do What Is Right

"But Mother, I love her!" Carl insisted. "I want to marry her!"

Brigit sighed. Her son was a grown man, but he was acting like a spoiled child who had been denied a new toy.

"It's wrong, Carl, and you know it," she repeated. "You already have a wife back home in Sweden, waiting for us to return from this pilgrimage. And Queen Joanna has a husband in Spain."

"But Joanna and I are so right for each other," Carl argued, more stubborn than ever. "Don't you want me to be happy?"

Brigit lost patience with her son. "You may be happy with her right now, but I know one thing. You cannot turn your back on your faith and expect to be happy for long. Think, Carl! For once in your life, think about what *God* wants. Remember your relationship with *Him*!"

Carl looked at her in disbelief. "I thought you loved me," he said.

Brigit took her son's hand in hers. "I do love you. And that is why I am begging you—not just for my sake, but for yours, and for Joanna's, too—to do the right thing."

"I'll never leave Joanna!" Carl shouted, and ran from the room.

Brigit wept silently. Then, she prayed for help.

Over the next week, as the little group of travelers waited for the weather to clear so that they could set sail for the Holy Land, Carl and Queen Joanna continued their love affair. Then, Carl fell ill with a high fever. Brigit cared for her son and continued to pray. One night, Carl began to speak to her.

"I was wrong . . .," he whispered, ". . . about Joanna."

Brigit put a cool cloth on his head. She wondered whether Carl had really changed his heart, or whether it was the fever talking. He seemed to understand her unspoken question, and smiled.

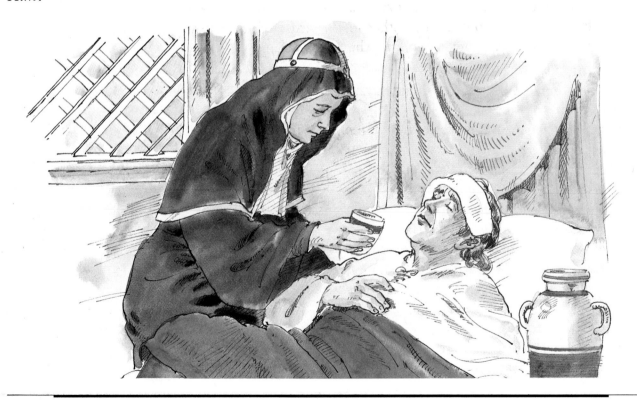

FAITH

"No, Mother, I made up my mind before I got sick," Carl said. "I want to do what is right. Joanna does, too. Thank . . . you."

In spite of Brigit's care, her son died soon after their conversation. Heartbroken, Brigit continued on her pilgrimage alone. But everywhere she went, she spoke the same words to all who would listen.

"For the love of God, turn away from sin," Brigit repeated. "Find your happiness in the Way of Christ."

A Covenant of Love

Brigit (known today as Saint Brigit of Sweden) never gave any advice that she herself did not follow. She lived by God's law because she loved God. She trusted in the Holy Spirit and in the gift of right judgment to sort through difficult decisions. She spoke the truth even when her son accused her of not loving him. And always, she kept in mind her relationship with God.

Through Baptism, we have that same relationship. God has made a *covenant* of love with us. God says, "I will be your God, and you will be My People"—not because we deserve it or earn it, but because God loves us. God has promised never to go back on His word, even when we do not keep our part of the agreement.

Time after time, our ancestors in faith, the Israelites, failed to live up to the covenant. Speaking through the *prophets*, God called them back *(Isaiah 55:68; Jeremiah 31:16–17; Hosea 14:2–3)*. Time after time, the people of Jesus' day—even His own friends and followers—forgot how much God loved them. Jesus showed them by His words and actions: through the parables of God's forgiveness *(Luke 15)*; through His welcome of repentant sinners *(Luke 7:36–50; John 8:1–11)*; and especially through His own suffering and death *(Romans 5:8–11)*.

Faith and Right Judgment

The Holy Spirit's gift of right judgment works with our faith in God's forgiving love to help us make good decisions. Through right judgment or counsel, we learn to be comfortable with a life that is full of choices and changes. We learn that it is OK to make honest mistakes—especially if we can own up to them and learn from them—and OK to ask for help.

In addition to helping us live with our own failings, the Holy Spirit's gift of right judgment helps us reach out to others in forgiveness and love. We begin to see that it is just as important to forgive as it is to ask forgiveness.

There will be times in your life when, like Saint Brigit's son, you may think that you are being forced to choose between being happy and living up to your part of God's covenant. The Holy Spirit's gift of right judgment can help you see where true happiness lies. It can help you live with yourself and with your choices. And with God's help, you may be able to be there for others when they are faced with difficult decisions.

The Forgiveness of Sins

God always loves us. We, on the other hand, are free to return that love or to reject it. The decision to reject God's love is called *sin*, from the Hebrew word that means "missing the mark."

In the Apostles' Creed, we declare that we believe in "the forgiveness of sin." In praying these words, we are reminding ourselves that God's love for us is unconditional. But we are also admitting that we are not perfect. We need forgiveness from God and from one another.

You cannot have reached your early teens without having some sense that sin exists and is very real. You have seen some of the ways that people can hurt one another through selfishness, greed, and carelessness. You have seen how lack of respect for God can result in the mistreatment of His creation. You certainly know what it is to feel sorrow for sin, and to want to begin again.

This knowledge and experience lies behind the need each one of us has to seek true *conversion*—to continually "turn our lives

Religious Vocabulary

Covenant A sacred, loving agreement or mutual relationship. God made a covenant with His people. Christian marriage is another kind of covenant relationship.

Prophets The wise men and women of the Old Testament who spoke for God and reminded people of the covenant.

Sin From the Hebrew for "missing the mark"; the deliberate choice to turn away from God's love, expressed in wrong action or failure to act in the right way.

Conversion Literally, "to turn around"; the process of bringing one's life into line with God's covenant of love.

Sacrament of Reconciliation The sacrament in which Catholics confess their sins to a priest, express their sorrow, promise to do better, and receive absolution or sacramental forgiveness. The sacrament of Reconciliation is required in cases of mortal sin, and strongly encouraged as a way to grow in faith.

around" so that we make choices and carry out actions with our covenant relationship in mind.

Throughout your life—and especially now, in preparation for Confirmation—you can make use of the *sacrament of Reconciliation* as a way to keep your relationship with God alive and growing. This sacrament is not just a place to seek forgiveness for mortal sin—although sacramental confession and absolution are necessary in order to return to a state of grace. In the sacrament of Reconciliation, you can find the strength to overcome bad habits and to face peer pressure. You can talk about your questions and problems, and receive good counsel. And, with the whole Catholic community, you can celebrate God's love in your life.

Think It Over/Write About It

1. How did Saint Brigit use the Holy Spirit's gift of right judgment?
2. Why are conversion and forgiveness important?
3. How do you feel about participating in the sacrament of Reconciliation? What do you think life would be like *without* this opportunity to celebrate conversion and forgiveness? In what ways could this sacrament be a help to you as you prepare for Confirmation? Throughout your life?
4. Think about one area of your life that is in need of conversion. Then, write a brief prayer asking God's help and forgiveness.

Choices and Consequences

The Holy Spirit's gift of right judgment builds on the decision-making skills that you can practice every day. For each of the situations below, list several possible ways you could respond (alternatives). Next to each alternative, list the probable consequences. Look over your lists carefully, and choose the alternative you think is the best decision in each case. Circle this alternative.

1. During a test, you notice that the person next to you is copying answers from your paper. This other student is really popular with your classmates. You aren't sure what to do.

Alternatives	**Consequences**

2. Your teacher has scheduled a field trip. At least one parent has to go along as a chaperone, or the trip will be cancelled. No one else is volunteering. You know your mother would probably enjoy going along, but field trips are never as much fun with her there. You wonder whether or not to ask her.

Alternatives	**Consequences**

3. Your friend has invited you to an all-day concert starring your favorite groups. Your grandparents, who have not seen you in over a year, are scheduled to be in town on a short visit the same day as the concert.

Alternatives	**Consequences**

Making Connections

Match the terms in Column B with the descriptions in Column A.
Write the correct letter on each line.

_____ 1. His life, death, and resurrection are the greatest signs of God's love.

_____ 2. The failure to return God's love.

_____ 3. People who speak for God and remind God's People of the covenant.

_____ 4. The gift of the Holy Spirit that helps us make good moral decisions.

_____ 5. The ability to make decisions based on insight, so they seem quick and simple.

_____ 6. Turning one's life around.

_____ 7. She used right judgment to help her son.

_____ 8. The sacrament that celebrates God's forgiving love.

_____ 9. A name for the gift of right judgment that reminds us of the importance of getting and giving good advice.

_____ 10. A sacred, loving agreement or mutual relationship.

a. conversion
b. Saint Brigit
c. right judgment
d. covenant
e. intuition
f. Reconciliation
g. Jesus Christ
h. sin
i. counsel
j. prophets

Vocabulary Review

Look up each of the following terms in the Glossary which begins on page 117. Then, use these terms in a short paragraph.

confession	covenant	Reconciliation
conversion	grace	sin

_____

_____

_____

_____

_____

An Examination of Conscience

In preparation for Confirmation, you should plan to celebrate the sacrament of Reconciliation with your classmates or your family, either as part of a parish penitential service or during the regularly scheduled times for confession. The examination of conscience printed here is based on the Ten Commandments, the sign of your covenant with God. Use these questions to help you ask God's forgiveness and grow in faith.

1. Do I really love God above all things? Do I let material things come between me and God?

2. Do I show respect for God's name? When I make promises, do I take them seriously?

3. Do I participate fully in the Mass on Sundays and holidays? Do I pray regularly? Do I make time for God in my life?

4. Do I contribute to my family's happiness? Do I obey my parents and give good example to my brothers and sisters? Do I have respect for older people and those in authority?

5. Do my actions show that I believe life is sacred? Do I take care of my body? Do I avoid movies and TV shows that take life cheaply or glorify violence?

6. Do I respect my sexuality as a gift from God? Do I respect the bodies of others? Am I modest in my thoughts, my words, and in the way I dress?

7. Do I use money and resources responsibly? Do I avoid cheating or stealing? Do I respect the budget limitations my family lives with?

8. Do I communicate openly, honestly, and respectfully with others—especially my family, my teachers, my friends? Do I gossip about others or "run them down"?

9. Do I respect the sacrament of Marriage? Do I show by my actions that my family is important to me? Am I jealous of the relationship my family members or friends have with others?

10. Am I envious of the things others have? Do I share what I have? Do I try to reach out to others?

Understanding and Right Judgment

Through the gift of understanding, we come to see ourselves, others, and life from God's point of view. We combine this insight with the Holy Spirit's gift of right judgment to make good decisions. Use the outline of this page to help you pray for the ability to grow in your covenant relationship with God. You can pray by yourself, with your classmates, or with your family.

Scripture Readings (Choose 1 or 2):
> Psalm 51:3–4, 9–14 (Prayer of repentance)
> Psalm 89:2–6 (God's everlasting covenant)
> Luke 10:21–24 (True understanding)
> Ephesians 5:1–10 (Living in the light of Christ)

Music: Choose a hymn, song, or piece of instrumental music that has meaning for you—one that speaks to the theme of your prayer. Sing or listen to the music.

Sharing Experience: Think about a time when you have experienced forgiveness and reconciliation. If you are praying with others, share your experience.

Prayer: Pray the following litany aloud.

Leader: For all the times we were too busy for one another . . .

   All: Lord, have mercy.

Leader: For all the times we were not faithful to what we believe . . .

   All: Christ, have mercy.

Leader: For all the times when we forgot our covenant with You . . .

   All: Lord, have mercy.

Leader: Let us pray.

   All: God, our Father, we are truly sorry for the times when we have not lived up to our covenant with You. We are also sorry for the good we did not do. Help us grow in love each day and to share with others. Help us to be more like Your Son, Jesus, through the gifts of Your Holy Spirit. Amen.

7

Journey of Faith

In This Chapter

- You will examine the nature of happiness and how it relates to your faith.
- You will learn more about the gift of wonder and awe.
- You will realize that the resurrection of Jesus calls us to new life in this world and in the next.

The Challenge

- To be happy
- To show by my life that the resurrection is real and makes a difference
- To continue growing in faith as someone who is comfortable with wonder and surprise

Something New

Teresa felt miserable. Her friend Abby would be away on a family vacation for another two weeks. Meanwhile, the days just dragged.

"There's nothing to do," Teresa complained to her mother. "I can't go to the movies by myself. And I know what you're going to say about books—but I'm too bored to read!"

"How about. . . ."

"Swimming?" Teresa finished her mother's question. "I've done that every day for the past three weeks. I'm turning into a prune."

Teresa's mother laughed. "You've got a problem, sweetie."

They were interrupted by the sound of the screen door slamming. "Who's home?" called Teresa's Grandpa Donnelly.

He caught sight of his granddaughter's dejected face. "What's the problem, kiddo?" he asked.

"I'm bored," Teresa dragged the words out, not even bothering to look up.

"Only one cure for that," Grandpa said briskly. "Pack a lunch. We're going to go exploring up on Granite Mountain."

Teresa smiled half-heartedly. "OK," she sighed. "I guess there's nothing better to do."

While Grandpa talked to her mom, Teresa made sandwiches and washed two apples. She packed the food in a cooler.

Grandpa drove to the edge of town. He turned his old truck onto the canyon road and wound through the woods toward Granite Mountain. Finally, they pulled off the road and parked beside a stream.

"Whenever *I* get bored, I come here," Grandpa told Teresa. "There's always something new to discover."

"Something new . . . in the middle of nowhere?" Teresa was doubtful. She loved her grandfather, but she wasn't a little kid anymore. A ride in the country was no big deal.

"You'll see," said Grandpa.

They ate lunch sitting on a flat rock in the sun. Then, Grandpa took two battered pie tins from the back of the truck.

"What are you doing?" Teresa asked, as she followed him downstream, picking her way carefully over the rocks.

"I'm going to teach you to pan for gold," Grandpa said.

"Oh, sure!" Teresa laughed out loud. "There's no gold up here!"

"You'd be surprised," was all Grandpa would say.

At a shallow place in the stream, he dug up some silt. He swished it back and forth in a pie pan, tilting the pan so the water and sand caught the light. He repeated this procedure several times. "See there," Grandpa said at last, pointing to the remaining silt. "These are gold flakes."

Teresa looked with amazement at the thin, sparkling line of particles. "You mean, they're real?" she breathed.

"Sure are," Grandpa grinned. Carefully, he picked the flakes out with tweezers and placed them in a plastic bottle. "It may take a while, but if you get an ounce of this stuff, it's worth a fair amount of money."

"Can I try?" In her eagerness, Teresa forgot to be bored.

"Just takes a little concentration, and knowing where to dig," said Grandpa, showing Teresa how to sift through the silt.

The afternoon passed quickly. Teresa never did find more than a few flakes of gold, but she had fun looking. She enjoyed the feel of the warm sun and the cool water, and the sight of the hawks circling high in the air.

"Grandpa, were you always like this?" Teresa asked as they drove home. "I mean . . . did you always know how to make ordinary things seem new and exciting?"

"No," he answered slowly. "Not always. After your Grandma died, I got so I didn't even want to get out of bed in the morning. Everything seemed sort of empty. But then I realized that life goes on—and it's just too precious to waste. I also figured out that it was up to me to make the most of my time. Now, I can be happy doing almost anything— or even doing nothing."

Teresa thought about his words. She held her little container of gold flakes up toward the windshield, where it caught the last rays of the sun.

"Grandpa," she asked quietly, "do you think I'll ever be happy like that?"

He patted her hand. "Sure, honey," he said with a nod. "It's like panning for gold. It just takes practice . . . and knowing where to dig."

Think It Over/Write About It

1. How did Teresa feel at the beginning of the day? Why did she feel differently at the end of the day?
2. What do you think Grandpa Donnelly meant when he said, "I figured out that it was up to me to make the most of my time"?
3. What things do you usually turn to when you are bored or unhappy?
4. Make a list of five things (people, events, places) that make you feel happy. Then, write your own definition of happiness.

Finding Happiness

Everyone wants to be happy, and yet—as Teresa learned—happiness can be hard to find. It seems to avoid us purposely, just when we are most in need. We can begin to think that we must do something really extraordinary in order to be happy.

That's why some people in our society think that money or alcohol or drugs will bring happiness. Some think that owning just the right "things"—a fancy car, jewelry, a stereo system with a CD player—is the key to happiness. Still others define happiness as having a boyfriend or girlfriend, getting better grades, or being invited to the "in" party of the year. "If only . . . ," these people are constantly saying. "If only I had this, or this happened, *then* I'd be happy."

Some people spend their whole lives chasing happiness but never finding it. The reason is simple: nothing outside us can *make* us happy. True happiness comes from within. It's something we choose to feel and to welcome—or to reject. That's what Grandpa Donnelly discovered after the death of his wife. It's what he taught Teresa.

Happiness is possible for us, even in difficult times, because God has given us the freedom to view life and all of its experiences in a positive way. From the most exciting and challenging occasion to the simplest everyday pleasure, God has surrounded us with opportunities to be interested, amazed, and joyful.

Wonder and Awe

Remember, if you can, how you reacted to the world as a very young child: excited by a snail that curled backward into its shell; amazed at the movement of puffy clouds across a blue sky; surprised, then delighted by a puppy that leaped into your lap. To a child, each of these experiences is new and marvelous. Unconsciously, without the words to describe it, a child is continually overwhelmed by the greatness of God.

The things that amaze and delight you today may be quite different, but as long as you retain the ability to feel joy, the ability to be surprised, you remain open to God's presence in your life.

In Baptism and Confirmation, the Holy Spirit gives us a special gift of openness to God—*the gift of wonder and awe*. In a way, this gift takes what is best about a child's unconscious response to God and to creation, and makes it conscious. Through the gift of wonder and awe, we know *why* we are happy. We recognize that behind every incredible sunset or friendly smile or peaceful moment is a

look and be our best for those we love and those who love us here and now, so the gift of wonder and awe calls us to respond to God's love with all that is best in ourselves.

Filled with the Spirit

In Confirmation, we celebrate the presence of the Holy Spirit in each member of the Catholic community. That presence is often marked by some very clear signs. A person who is filled with the Holy Spirit is somehow more "alive"—more hopeful, more lively, more willing to face hard times cheerfully. A person who is truly Spirit-filled is also someone others want to spend time with.

Unfortunately, as some young people grow up, they tend to (as Saint Paul says) "stifle the Spirit." They grow indifferent and careless. Like Teresa at the beginning of the story, they are easily bored and have a hard time believing that things will never change for the better. Indifferent and careless people may try to fool themselves into thinking that their behavior is cool or mature. But, in the long run, their boredom becomes whining, and their indifference becomes a total inability to act. And that's no fun to have happen—or to be around.

The Holy Spirit's gift of wonder and awe works for us the way Teresa's day with her grandfather worked for her. When we are most tempted to give up or to believe that nothing good will ever happen, God breaks through into our lives. We begin to see the

God who loves us, and who made us for one reason only: to be happy with Him forever.

The Spirit's gift of wonder and awe works with all the other gifts, especially the gift of reverence, to remind us to be very careful of all life. Through wonder and awe, we read all the delightful surprises in our lives as love letters from God. And, just as we want to

■ ■ ■

Religious Vocabulary

The gift of wonder and awe The gift of the Holy Spirit that helps us remain open to the surprising, delightful, loving presence of God in our lives, and to respond with goodness and love.

wonderful possibilities that are present in every day—like tiny flecks of gold in the mud of the riverbank.

As you prepare for Confirmation, you can call on the Holy Spirit in prayer to help you fight indifference, boredom, and careless-ness. You can ask the Holy Spirit to help you grow up—without growing out of the curios-ity and delight of childhood. By cooperating with the Spirit's gift of wonder and awe, you can be continually amazed at the goodness that is present in your life.

Think It Over/Write About It

1. Think about an experience you have had that you might describe as "wonderful" or "awesome." How is God present in that experience?
2. When was the last time you were genuinely surprised? Why do you think some people act as though it's "immature" or "uncool" to be surprised and delighted?
3. What things in our society keep people from fully experiencing the Holy Spirit's gift of wonder and awe?
4. List three or four qualities you associate with someone you enjoy being around. How do these qualities reflect the presence of the Holy Spirit? Are they qualities you want to develop in yourself as you continue to grow?

The Wonder of Jesus

Jesus lived the gift of wonder and awe through every moment. He was never bored or uncaring. He never lost the perfect innocence of childhood. Jesus even pointed to children as examples of those most directly in touch with God's amazing love. "Let the children come to Me, and do not prevent them," Jesus said, "for the kingdom of heaven belongs to such as these" *(Matthew 19:14)*.

The parables of Jesus are about ordinary people and events, but they never failed to surprise His listeners with a new way of looking at things. A hated Samaritan becomes a hero *(Luke 10:29–37)*. A landowner pays all his workers the same wages—even those who only work one hour *(Matthew 20:1–16)*. A shepherd leaves ninety-nine well-behaved sheep behind to go looking for the one who strays *(Luke 15:4–7)*.

At the core of these parables is a simple message: our God is a God who loves and respects all people. God is not indifferent or uncaring. God gives everyone a second chance. God Himself will search for us when we are lost.

Faith and Wonder

It would be a mistake to think that the gift of wonder and awe is meant only for happy times. That wouldn't be much of a gift, because most of us find it fairly easy to see God's goodness when things are going smoothly.

Jesus showed us how to look for God's goodness, not only in the delight of childhood, but also in the depths of fear and pain. In a way, His very life was a parable of God's great love. When Jesus told His friends that He would suffer and die, they did not understand. No one expected this kind of ending for God's Chosen One. The Apostles were so shaken by the arrest and crucifixion of Jesus that all but one of them, John, abandoned Him in death. And yet there was still one surprise left.

The *resurrection* of Jesus is the greatest surprise the world has ever experienced. It changed once and for all the way we look at death. Jesus' resurrection transformed something fearful into something wonderful, something awesome.

Our faith in the resurrection of Jesus is faith in God's unending goodness. This faith explains why another name for the Holy Spirit's gift of wonder and awe is *fear of the Lord*. The "fear" we're talking about is not hopelessness or dread, but a healthy respect for God's power. The gift of fear of the Lord reminds us never to underestimate our God.

Life Everlasting

Because of Jesus, it is possible for us to believe that we, too, will experience everlasting life. We see death as an end to human suffering, and the beginning of a new life. We believe the promise of Jesus, that "whoever lives and believes in Me will never die" *(John 11:26)*.

This faith in the promise is what is behind the words we speak in the Apostles' Creed: we "believe in the resurrection of the body and life everlasting."

We believe that our happiness after death—the happiness for which we were created—depends on our response to God's love here on earth. If our response has been good and loving, if we have sincerely tried to live as Jesus did, then our trust in God's

goodness leads us to believe we will be welcomed into the *kingdom of God*, which we call *heaven*. Heaven is not a place, but a state of indescribable happiness. Perhaps Saint Paul said it best: "Eye has not seen and ear has not heard . . . what God has prepared for those who love Him" *(1 Corinthians 2:9)*.

The "resurrection of the body" refers to our belief that at some point the world as we know it will come to an end. This event is sometimes called the *parousia*, or Second Coming of Christ. It cannot be predicted, just as heaven cannot be described. For those who believe in Jesus, the parousia will indeed be a wonderful and awesome event. God's kingdom of perfect peace, love, and justice will come at last.

Little Resurrections

An eighth-grade boy, saddened because he thinks he is the only person not invited to a popular classmate's party, receives a hand-delivered invitation from the classmate herself. A seventh-grade girl, sure her father's business trip will keep him from attending her piano recital, looks up to see him standing in the back row. A family, miserable because their dog ran away during a storm, wakes up to find the dog asleep on the front porch.

These moments of life when we experience a rebirth of joy and energy might be called "little resurrections." They are glimpses of the wonders God has in store for us through all eternity. These little resurrections awaken in us a sense of longing for the time when we will be face-to-face with God. Without faith, without the Holy Spirit's gift of wonder and awe, these little resurrections might pass us by. Saint Bernadette, a peasant girl who lived in nineteenth-century France, knew how important the little resurrections can be.

A Place of Wonder

"Hurry up!" Bernadette's brother called impatiently from across the field. "We're going to miss dinner!"

"I'm coming," Bernadette called back. Hastily, she picked up another bare branch and added it to her pack. A gust of cold winter wind almost knocked her over.

Then the wheezing began. Dropping her load of firewood, Bernadette clutched her throat and tried to gulp in the freezing air. She sank down on the riverbank, still struggling to breathe.

"Oh, Bernadette, not your asthma again!" her sister, running back, cried with dismay. "Here," she added sympathetically, "I'll take your bundle. Follow us when you can."

Bernadette managed to nod. As her sister and brother headed for home, she tried to steady her breathing by staring at the flowing water in the riverbed. Her eyes took in the

stubble of the field and the dark pile of rocks that towered at one end. Most people, she knew, would find this place ugly. But Bernadette found it fascinating. There was always something new to see and discover—a field

■ ■ ■

Religious Vocabulary

Resurrection The rising of the body to be reunited with the immortal (undying) soul after death. We celebrate the resurrection of Jesus on Easter Sunday. His resurrection enables us to believe that God's power is greater than suffering and death, and that we, too, will share in eternal life.

Fear of the Lord A traditional name for the Holy Spirit's gift of wonder and awe. This name for the gift reminds us not to underestimate God's power and love.

Kingdom of God The phrase Jesus used to describe God's powerful action in time and eternity. As Christians, we believe that the kingdom of God is both present "in our

midst" as a promise, and yet to come as a state of perfect happiness, peace, and justice.

Heaven Another name for the timeless or eternal kingdom of God; the state of perfect happiness with God.

Parousia From the Greek word for "presence" or "arrival"; the end of the world as we know it; the Second Coming of Christ.

Immaculate Conception A title of Mary that describes our belief that she was free from all sin from the very beginning of her life. We celebrate the feast of the Immaculate Conception on December 8.

mouse scurrying through the wheatstalks, a bird diving for a fish, cloud shadows playing on the cliff face. Bernadette loved this place, and she was grateful that gathering firewood gave her an excuse to come here.

Slowly, she got up and began to walk toward the rocks, hoping they would shelter her from the icy wind. The walk tired her, and once again she sank to her knees. Suddenly, Bernadette found herself looking up at the shining white dress of a beautiful lady.

Bernadette was too astonished to say anything. But her wheezing stopped at once, and she was filled with joy and a deep sense of peace.

After that day, Bernadette saw the Lady seventeen times. The Lady told Bernadette, "I am the *Immaculate Conception*." No one believed the little peasant girl, but curious people began to assemble near the rocky cliff. One day, following the directions of the beautiful Lady no one else could see, Bernadette dug with her hands in the dirt. Up came a spring of water with the power to heal. This miracle, and Bernadette's own simple honesty,

convinced the people that Bernadette's "Lady" was Mary, the Mother of Jesus.

Today, there is a church at Lourdes, and the spring still flows. Each year, thousands of people visit this shrine of Mary, to pray for the gift of healing and to receive the miracle of new life.

Think It Over/Write About It

1. How did Jesus demonstrate the gift of wonder and awe in His life and teaching?
2. How do you feel when you think about death? About eternity? About heaven? Is it possible to live with these realities even when we do not understand everything about them?
3. How did Saint Bernadette use the gift of wonder and awe to experience a "little resurrection"? How did her use of this gift help to make others happy?
4. Think of one area of your life in which you might be tempted to "underestimate" God's power and love. How can the Holy Spirit's gift of wonder and awe (or fear of the Lord) help you resist the temptation to give in to despair or hopelessness?

Walking by Faith

The early Christians sometimes described themselves as "Easter people," or "walking Alleluias," as a sign of the wonder and awe they experienced through the resurrection of Jesus. We are challenged to be Easter people, too—to find new meaning in life and in death, and be people who are continually growing in hope and happiness.

Read and reflect on the following passage from a letter of Saint Paul. Then, as part of a small group, do one of the suggested activities.

> We know that when this earthly tent in which we dwell is destroyed, we have a dwelling prepared for us by God, a dwelling in the heavens, not made by hands but to last forever. Therefore, we continue to be confident. We know that while we dwell in the body we are away from the Lord. We walk by faith, not by sight. This being so, we make it our aim to please the Lord whether we are with Him or away from Him *(2 Corinthians 5:1–9)*.

Activities

1. Choose a partner. One person is blindfolded (or closes his or her eyes). The other person leads him or her on a short walk. Then, switch roles. Talk about how you felt. Was it easier to lead or to be led? Were you afraid? What did this exercise teach you about trust?

2. Construct a mural with your group's ideas about what heaven will be like. Include written reflections, poetry, personal drawings, or photos clipped from magazines. Share your mural with the class.

3. Prepare and practice a short skit representing the experience of a "little resurrection." Perform your skit for the rest of the class.

4. Discuss the following questions in your group. If possible, have each group member ask these same questions of one or two family members or friends. Summarize the responses and share them with the class.

   a. Why is life meaningful to you?
   b. If you knew the world would end one year from today, would you change your life in any way? If so, how? If not, why not?
   c. How does faith help you?

True or False

Circle the T if the statement is true. Circle the F if the statement is false.

1. Having the right things is the best way to be happy.   T   F
2. Jesus taught that only adults could go to heaven.   T   F
3. The Holy Spirit's gift of wonder and awe is not only meant for good times.   T   F
4. There is life after death.   T   F
5. The everlasting life promised by Jesus means that Catholics will never have to experience suffering or bodily death.   T   F
6. Heaven is one name for the kingdom of God.   T   F
7. Fear of the Lord is another name for the Holy Spirit's gift of wonder and awe.   T   F
8. According to Jesus, the end of the world will happen in the year 2000.   T   F
9. The resurrection of Jesus Christ changes the way Christians look at life and death.   T   F
10. The gift of wonder and awe is fine for young children, but mature Christians are not surprised or excited by many things.   T   F

Vocabulary Review

Look up each of the following words in the Glossary which begins on page 117. Then, choose three words and use each one in a complete sentence.

fear of the Lord	parousia
Immaculate Conception	resurrection
kingdom of God	wonder and awe

1. _____

_____

2. _____

_____

3. _____

_____

Wonderful Promises

As you already know, the sacrament of Confirmation is closely related to Baptism. In Confirmation, you are asked to *confirm*—or give your personal consent to—the promises that were made for you at Baptism. Each one of these promises deals with faith, the way Catholic Christians look at reality.

To prepare for your Confirmation and to increase your understanding of these promises, ask yourself the following questions. Try to look at each faith-statement with the eyes of wonder and awe. You may want to talk about these questions with your family and your sponsor, and share any new insights you have with your classmates.

- What does it mean to reject Satan, all his works, and all his empty promises?
- How have I experienced God as an almighty and loving Father, Creator of heaven and earth?
- What difference does it make in my life that Jesus Christ is God's only Son, that He was born of the Virgin Mary, that He was crucified, died, and was buried, rose from the dead, and is now seated at the right hand of the Father?
- Who is the Holy Spirit? How have I experienced this Spirit as the Giver of Life?
- What is the holy catholic Church? What is my part in the Church?
- What is the communion of saints?
- What is the forgiveness of sins? What does it mean to me?
- What is the resurrection of the body? How does this belief make a difference in my life here on earth?
- What is life everlasting? Do I want to choose it? What will make life everlasting real for me?

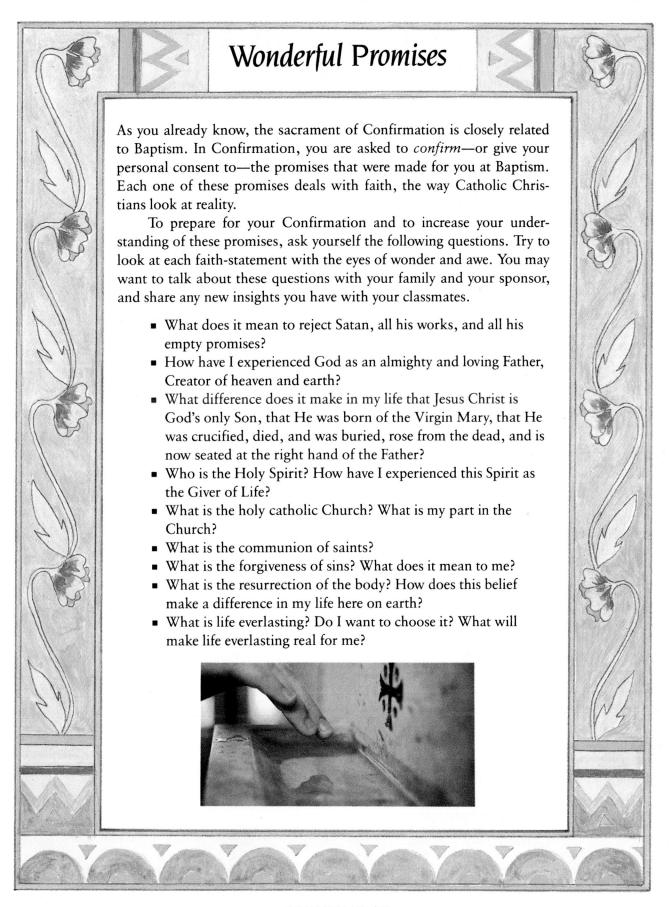

Praise to You!

Saint Francis of Assisi is well known for his love of God's creation. Yet few people know that—even in his singing, laughter, and childish delight—Francis suffered from times of terrible depression. He struggled and prayed, and, through the Holy Spirit's gift of wonder and awe, Francis began to see God's goodness shining through. Inspired by one of these experiences of "little resurrection," Francis composed one of the first poems in the Italian language—the beautiful prayer known as the Canticle of the Creatures.

In this poem, Francis calls all of God's creatures his "brothers and sisters." You can use the words of this prayer to praise God, to meditate on the wonders of God's creation, and to ask for God's help in facing your own difficult times.

Praise be to You, Creator God, in all Your creatures, especially in shining Brother Sun, who lights up the sky. Beautiful is he, and radiant with splendor. Of You, Most High, he is a sign.

Praised be my Lord for Sister Moon and for the stars. In heaven You have formed them, clear and precious and fair.

Praised be my Lord for Brother Wind, and for the air and clouds and fair skies and every kind of weather, by which You give Your creatures nourishment.

Praised be my Lord for Sister Water, who is helpful and humble, precious and pure.

Praised be my Lord for Brother Fire, by whom You light the darkness. Fair is he, and joyful and strong.

Praised be my Lord for our Sister, Mother Earth, who sustains and keeps us, bringing forth rich fruit and grass and flowers bright.

And praised be my Lord for shining Sister Death. Blessed are those whom she finds doing Your most holy will, for the second death shall not harm them.

Bless the Lord, and give Him thanks!

8

Indwelling Spirit

In This Chapter

- You will learn more about what it means to live in the Holy Spirit.
- You will take a closer look at the connection between Baptism and Confirmation.
- You will realize that all members of the Church are called to follow Jesus and to grow in holiness.

The Challenge

- To translate my beliefs and values into action
- To see myself as a person faithful to the creed and willing to keep growing in faith
- To welcome the renewing presence of the Holy Spirit and the support of the Catholic community in Confirmation

A New Start

Kristin raced up to Michelle and grabbed her arm. "Did you hear where we're going for our Christian service field trip?" she whispered dramatically.

Everything about Kristin was dramatic, but Michelle couldn't imagine what was so thrilling about a religion-class outing. "Where?" she asked, calmly.

"Circle X Ranch!" Michelle hissed, still whispering. "And you know who's staying *there*!"

Michelle knew. Circle X Ranch was a juvenile detention home in the hills above the lake. Jeremy Todd, a boy a year older than Michelle, was being held there. Jeremy had lived next door to Michelle. They had been friends, but that seemed like a long time ago. Now, Michelle's heart sank.

"So I guess everybody's talking about me again, right?" she asked bitterly. Kristin shook her head so hard that her glasses nearly flew off, but Michelle knew her friend was just trying to protect her.

The year before, Michelle had been nominated for seventh-grade class president. With the other candidates, she had been waiting to be interviewed by the student government moderator, Mr. Hoff. That same morning, news of Jeremy's arrest spread like wildfire through the school. Police officers even showed up to search his locker.

Instead of being asked her views on student activities and school spirit, Michelle found herself being questioned about Jeremy. She was already nervous about talking to Mr. Hoff, and when he asked whether she knew Jeremy, Michelle just stammered.

"He is your friend, isn't he?" demanded Mr. Hoff.

"We . . . uh, we walk to school together sometimes," Michelle managed to answer. "But he's an eighth grader. I mean, I don't talk to him that much."

By the time Mr. Hoff got around to asking questions about school, it was no use. Michelle had forgotten all her bright ideas. And the next day, she learned that Mr. Hoff had not approved her nomination.

That's when the rumors started. According to the story going around school, Jeremy had stolen $1,000 from an apartment in his building. He had been caught by the owner, but two other kids had escaped. To her horror, Michelle heard that *she* was rumored to be one of the other kids. Some people even said Michelle had the stolen money!

It had taken nearly a year for the rumors to fade. All those months, Michelle had worked harder than ever on her studies. She had ignored the hurtful things people whispered behind her back, hiding her tears from everyone but Kristin. And now, just because of the field trip, it was going to start all over again.

The day of the trip, Mr. Peterson, the teacher, explained what would happen. The students would be divided into small groups. Each group would be joined by some of the kids from the detention camp, and a counselor. They would spend some time talking together and then share lunch.

On the bus ride up through the hills, Michelle could hear the whispers building. One boy yelled, "Hey, Michelle! Are you gonna pass Jeremy his share of the money today?"

Michelle bit her lip to keep the tears back. "I want to be in Jeremy's group," she called out to Mr. Peterson in a firm, clear voice. It was more like a dare than a request, and, after a minute, Mr. Peterson nodded. Nobody said another word until the bus reached the ranch.

Michelle found herself in a group with about a third of her religion class, Jeremy, and ten other kids from the camp. The counselor asked for introductions.

When it was Jeremy's turn to talk, he said, "I know most of you already. Some of you, like Michelle, used to be my friends. Last year, I broke into a neighbor's apartment. Nobody else was involved. It was just me, trying to show off to some older kids. Living here has taught me how my actions can hurt myself and others.

"I'm sorry for what I did," Jeremy added quietly. "I hope when I come back to school I can get a new start."

There wasn't time for anyone to comment on what Jeremy had said. The counselor moved on to the next person.

When the session ended, the kids from Michelle's school and from the detention center paired off, formed small groups, and headed for the cafeteria.

Michelle and Kristin, walking with their classmates, passed Jeremy. He was standing alone. Michelle took a deep breath, and grinned at Jeremy. "Come on," she said.

He hesitated. Michelle could hear the whispers starting up again, kids who hadn't been in their group still wondering about Michelle's "connection" to Jeremy's crime. She grabbed Jeremy's hand. "You don't want to eat alone," she told him. "And besides," Michelle added, as Jeremy shyly joined the little group of kids, "you aren't the only one around here who needs a new start!"

Think It Over/Write About It

1. How can rumors or false stories damage a person's spirit?
2. Why do you think Michelle demanded to be placed in Jeremy's group?
3. What did Michelle mean by the last thing she said to Jeremy? What do you think Jeremy and Michelle will talk about at lunch? How can the other kids at school help both Jeremy and Michelle to get a new start?
4. Think of a time when you stood up for what you believed. Write about why you did it, and how you felt.

Beliefs and Actions

For a year, Michelle had worked hard in school and tried to become a better person. She cared what her classmates thought about her, which is why the false rumors about her involvement in Jeremy's crime hurt so much.

On the day of the field trip, Michelle took a new step. She reached out to Jeremy in a gesture of forgiveness, knowing that it meant risking the reputation she had worked so hard to rebuild.

Michelle was able to take her actions one step beyond what other people consider to be right or fair. Certainly, Michelle had been

treated unfairly—by her classmates and by Mr. Hoff—because of her friendship with Jeremy. Most people might think it would be only fair for Michelle to be resentful and to avoid Jeremy. But she used her good judgment and responded positively to the call of the Holy Spirit—the call to take the extra step.

The ability to act on our beliefs and values, to "put everything together," is called *integrity*. People who have integrity are known for "practicing what they preach"—living out the values they talk about. And while integrity itself is not one of the traditional gifts of the Holy Spirit, it is a necessary force or quality which helps us to live "in the Spirit" and to make use of all the gifts the Spirit has given us.

Attitudes of Integrity

The integrity involved in living our Christian faith is made up of two basic attitudes. One of these attitudes is *love*. Christlike love means that we respect the rights of others, as fellow children of God, to the things they need to live a decent life—the basic physical needs such as food, shelter, a job, money, peace. This love also includes concern for the psychological and spiritual needs of others. We believe that all people need attention, acceptance, and a sense of belonging.

The second basic attitude of integrity is *responsibility*. A sense of responsibility keeps us from being indifferent and apathetic toward the suffering of others. It can make us sensitive to situations where people are deprived of basic rights. And it can help us move beyond a simple idea of what's right—defined as what's fair or right for *me*—to a larger understanding of the common good.

Michelle left herself open to both of these attitudes in her meeting with Jeremy. As a result, she acted with integrity.

Growing in integrity as a witness to Jesus is the special task of those who receive the sacrament of Confirmation. This means believing in God's love and trying to share that love with others. It also means witnessing, or telling others about Jesus, when the opportunity presents itself. But above all, growth in integrity and Christian witness means trying to live and act according to Gospel values.

Fruit of the Holy Spirit

How can we know when we are truly living in the Spirit? How can we know that we are using the Spirit's gifts to their full potential? Jesus answered these questions with this statement: "Every good tree bears good fruit, and a rotten tree bears bad fruit. A good tree cannot bear bad fruit, nor can a rotten tree bear good fruit. . . . By their fruits you will know them" *(Matthew 7:17–18, 20)*. Jesus was not just describing a fact of nature. He was saying that each of us will be known and judged by our "fruit"—the way we act for all to see.

Saint Paul explains it even more clearly in a letter to the Christians of Asia Minor. He wrote that people who do not follow the Holy

Spirit can be recognized by their behavior. They are quarrelsome, hateful, jealous, and selfish. Each of these unChristian ways of acting is called a *vice*.

■ ■ ■

Religious Vocabulary

Integrity The ability to act in accord with one's beliefs.

Vices and virtues Vices are bad habits or ways of acting. Virtues are good habits or ways of acting. Growing in faith means practicing virtues and avoiding vices.

Fruit of the Spirit Qualities that indicate the presence of the Holy Spirit in one's life. Traditionally, these twelve qualities are: love (or charity), joy, peace, patience, kindness, generosity, faithfulness, gentleness (or modesty), self-control (or continency), goodness (or benignity), long-suffering (or longanimity), and chastity.

In the same letter, Paul identifies the qualities associated with those who do follow the Holy Spirit. They will act with "love, joy, peace, patience, kindness, generosity, faithfulness, gentleness, and self-control" *(Galatians 5:22)*. Each of these Christlike behaviors is a *virtue*. Together with goodness, long-suffering, and chastity, these twelve qualities are collectively known as the *fruit of the Holy Spirit*. When our actions are marked by these virtues—when we "bear good fruit"—we are acting with integrity in response to the Spirit's gifts.

Think It Over/Write About It

1. List the things you believe to be basic physical, psychological, and spiritual needs for every human being. When is a time when you have responded to those needs?
2. What opportunities do you have to witness to your faith in Jesus Christ?
3. What is a "good fruit" in your life that tells you that you are responding to the gifts of the Holy Spirit? If you can think of a "bad fruit," quietly ask the Spirit's help in overcoming this vice.
4. There is an old saying: "Actions speak louder than words." Tell what this saying means to you, and whether you agree with it. Then, talk about how this saying relates to the sacrament of Confirmation.

The Sacrament of Confirmation

As you have learned, your Confirmation celebrates the completion of your Baptism. This "completion," however, is not an ending, but a *fullness*. Because Confirmation is the last of the sacraments of initiation you will receive, what you will celebrate is "the end of the beginning."

In a way, Confirmation is like an autumn harvest festival. It celebrates the blossoming and fruitfulness of the seeds of faith planted in Baptism. And just as a harvest is important not just for the fruit that will be eaten immediately, but also for the seeds that will promise additional riches in years to come, so your Confirmation celebrates everything you are and everything you are yet to become in faith. Faith is alive and working within you, and you are living in the Spirit.

This living in the Spirit is what the Catholic community celebrates in Confirmation. We celebrate the Spirit *in action*, visible and present in our midst—in the life of Jesus, in the whole history of the Catholic community, and in each individual member of the Church.

The Rite

Looking one last time at *how* we celebrate the sacrament of Confirmation is a good way to keep mind and prepare for *what* we celebrate. There are three specific parts of the rite of Confirmation that clearly show the meaning of the sacrament.

(1) The Presence of the Bishop The bishop of your diocese is the official representative of the universal Church. Although the bishop was symbolically present in the use of the blessed *chrism* at your Baptism, most likely he was not personally present. For Confirmation, however, the bishop is the ordinary or normal minister. As a successor of the Apostles of Jesus, the bishop connects your experience of the Holy Spirit to the outpouring of that same Spirit upon the Apostles at Pentecost. As a representative of the wider Church, the bishop formally welcomes you to a fuller degree of membership and challenges you to become involved in the life of the Church.

As Pope John Paul II, the Bishop of Rome, said to a Confirmation class of Italian young people, "The bishops are the successors of the Apostles. I myself am the successor of Saint Peter. We say to you: You must help us: when the bishop administers Confirmation, he says: I am counting on *you*. Christ needs *you*. His Church needs *you*!"

(2) The Laying on of Hands You already know that one gesture that forms a special

part of the rite of Confirmation is the laying on of hands. This, too, is a tie to the apostolic community. We know that the laying on of hands was one way in which the Apostles called on God to send His Spirit to new Christians. "Peter and John . . . went down and prayed for them, that they might receive the Holy Spirit. . . . Then they laid hands on them and they received the Holy Spirit" *(Acts 8:15–17)*.

The laying on of hands, as you have learned, is a sign of *commissioning*, or sending forth to do God's work. That is why this gesture is used in the ordination of deacons and priests. But it is also an ancient sign of *blessing*, or calling down God's grace, and of healing or *forgiveness*, which is why this gesture is also used in the sacraments of Reconciliation and Anointing.

In Confirmation, all these aspects—commissioning, blessing, healing, and strengthening—can be seen in the laying on of hands. It is during this gesture that the bishop prays that you will receive the gifts of the Holy Spirit in all their fullness.

(3) Anointing with Chrism You have already learned the significance of anointing in the sacraments of Baptism and Confirmation. The signing with blessed oil strengthens you for the spiritual journey ahead and reminds you of your baptismal call to follow Jesus as "priest, prophet, and king." But it is also important to note that early people also used heavy oil as a *seal* to protect and coat precious objects, and to bind things together. This "sealing" of your baptismal commitment is the special significance of Confirmation. That is why, as the bishop anoints you with chrism, he speaks the most important words of the rite, words that have come to us from the poetic liturgies of the Eastern rites: "Be sealed with the Gift of the Holy Spirit."

The anointing of Confirmation shows the world that God has chosen you in a special way to follow Christ, to be a member of the Church, and to grow each day in holiness.

The Call to Holiness

To grow in holiness means that we sincerely try to respond to the Holy Spirit acting in our lives. It means that we continually work to become more like Christ in our every action.

Some confirmed Catholics choose to live out their call to holiness as a priest, a religious brother, or a sister. Most Catholics live out their call to holiness through marriage and family life. Still others seek holiness as single men and women. In each of these *vocations*, we are challenged to live as Jesus asked His followers to live. We are asked to be loving and responsible members of His Church.

In spite of what some people think, the call to holiness does not require extraordinary talent or training. As the life of Saint John Neumann shows us, sometimes the most ordinary people can be holy.

Ordinary Holiness

John stood nervously before the desk of the seminary rector. He was about to learn the results of his final exam. If he had passed, he would be ordained a priest. If he had failed, he would be required to study for another long year.

The rector looked up from his papers and frowned. "I'm afraid I have bad news for you, John," he said.

John's face fell. "I failed the test," he whispered.

"On the contrary," the rector replied. "You passed with high marks. But you will not be ordained."

John was both shocked and confused. "But if I passed. . . ."

"The decision was not mine, but the bishop's," the rector explained gently. "Czechoslovakia has all the priests it needs at this time, and the bishop has decided not to ordain anyone else. You must return home."

John was too numb to reply. None of this seemed fair. He felt himself growing angry, but he understood that he had no choice. John packed his bags and went home.

"If God wants you to be a priest, you will be a priest," John's mother said with sympathy.

"But how?" John asked. It was a question he repeated every day as his frustration grew.

"Find some place where you will be needed as a priest," his mother advised. "Perhaps you should go to America."

Two weeks later, with only a few coins in his pocket, John set sail for New York City. He had no idea what he would do once he got there. He only knew that he wanted to serve God as a priest.

The bishop of New York welcomed John and ordained him. Immediately, Father John was sent to upstate New York, where there was no priest for 900 miles. There, John

■ ■ ■

Religious Vocabulary

Chrism Pure olive oil mixed with balsam (a fragrant spice) and blessed by the bishop. Chrism is used in the sacraments of Baptism and Confirmation. It differs from the unscented oils, also blessed by the bishop, that are used to anoint catechumens and the sick.

Vocation A word that literally means "calling"; the call from God to live out our Christian commitment—to grow in holiness and to serve others—in a particular way. Marriage, priesthood, religious life, and the single life are all examples of vocation.

served the German immigrants in very ordinary ways. He celebrated Mass, visited the sick, taught religion classes, trained teachers, and spent many hours just talking to the people in their own language.

In 1852, John was made the fourth bishop of Philadelphia. Bishop John did what most bishops of his time did. He built churches and schools. He wrote two catechsims, or books of religious instruction. He taught Confirmation classes. And he continued to spend time with his people.

John Neumann died in 1860, at the age of 51. In 1921, Pope Benedict XV raised him to the first level of sainthood. Some people protested that John was too ordinary to be a saint. But Pope Benedict knew better. "Even the most simple works," he said, "he performed with faithfulness to God's Spirit, spell holiness."

In 1977, John Neumann was canonized. He was the third person from the United States to receive this honor.

Think It Over/Write About It

1. What does the sacrament of Confirmation celebrate?
2. What is the significance, in the Confirmation rite, of (a) the bishop's presence? (b) the laying on of hands? (c) the annointing with chrism?
3. How could Saint John Neumann be a model for confirmed Catholics?
4. Think about the particular vocation that is most attractive to you at this time in your life. Why do you feel drawn to this way of living out your call to holiness? Can you see the positive qualities of other vocations? Write a brief prayer asking Jesus for help in living out your call to holiness.

Spirit Profile

Throughout your preparation for Confirmation, you have been
learning more about what it means to be a Spirit-filled person.
But it's important to remember that the gifts of the Spirit and the
fruit of the Spirit are not magical abilities that will suddenly
appear in your life at Confirmation. You have been practicing
these gifts and expressing the fruit of the Spirit all along, ever
since Baptism. Confirmation affirms your willingness to take
responsibility for these gifts, to let the fruit of the Spirit shine
forth in everything you do.

Look over the two lists below. Then, spend some time
evaluating your own actions over the past year or so. For each area
listed, write about how you have used one gift of the Holy Spirit
or shown one fruit of the Spirit. You may talk about what you
have written with your famly, your sponsor, or your classmates.

Gifts of the Holy Spirit	Fruit of the Holy Spirit	
Wisdom	Love	Faithfulness
Understanding	Joy	Gentleness
Right Judgment	Peace	Self-Control
Courage	Patience	Goodness
Knowledge	Kindness	Long-Suffering
Reverence	Generosity	Chastity
Wisdom and Awe		

At Home

_____

_____

At School

_____

_____

With My Friends

_____

_____

With Someone in Need

_____

_____

Summing Up

The following questions will help you reflect on what you have learned during this time of preparation, and on how you feel about being confirmed. Use a separate sheet of paper or your journal or notebook to answer them as honestly as possible. Be prepared to share your answers.

1. What one new thing did you learn about yourself that most impressed you?

2. What one new thing did you learn about your faith that most impressed you?

3. Did any of your ideas about yourself or about your faith change during this preparation time? If so, how?

4. Share one part of your faith that you got a new insight into through this time of preparation.

5. Did you read, hear, or experience anything unexpected during this time of preparation? If so, what was it? How did it affect you?

6. What have the sacraments of Eucharist and Reconciliation meant to you during this time?

7. How have you used your skills and talents in Christian service? How might you continue to use them after Confirmation?

8. What has your prayer life been like during this time of preparation?

9. What does the Mass mean to you right now? Has its meaning changed for you during this time of preparation?

10. Share one way in which you feel you have grown in faith during this time.

11. Give examples of ways in which you've taken on more responsibility at home, in your parish, or in your community during this time.

12. Do you think you are ready to become a full member of the Church through the sacrament of Confirmation? Why or why not?

Vocabulary Review

Look up each of the following terms in the Glossary which begins on page 117. Then, use these terms in a short paragraph.

chrism	mission	vocation
holiness	virtues	witness

_____

_____

_____

_____

Making a Confirmation Shield

Heraldry is the art of creating signs and symbols that identify a person or a family. In heraldry, a shield is one of the principal symbols of identity. The designs and colors of a shield say something about the person who wears, carries, or displays it.

Because the Holy Spirit helps you in many ways to grow in your Catholic identity, you may want to make a shield to wear or carry at your Confirmation. A pattern is given here. In each of the four sections, draw a symbol representing your Catholic experiences and values. Practice on a piece of paper first; then, transfer your final drawings to this pattern or to a simple cloth banner. Some ideas for things to symbolize are:

- the gift of the Holy Spirit you most identify with at this time;
- the fruit of the Holy Spirit you would most like others to see in you;
- one way God has acted in your life in the past;
- one way you would like to give Christian witness in the future.

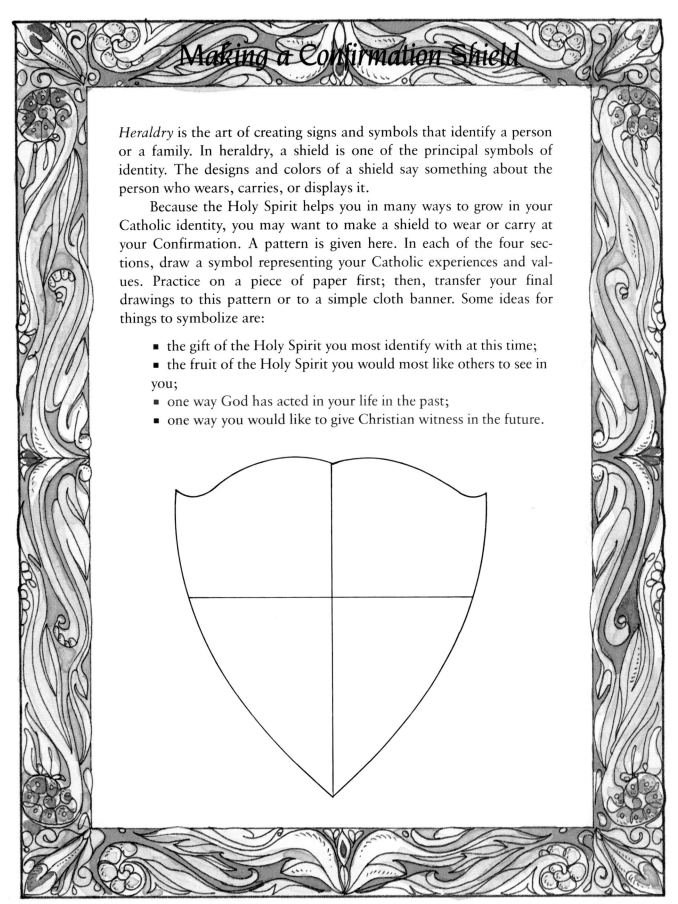

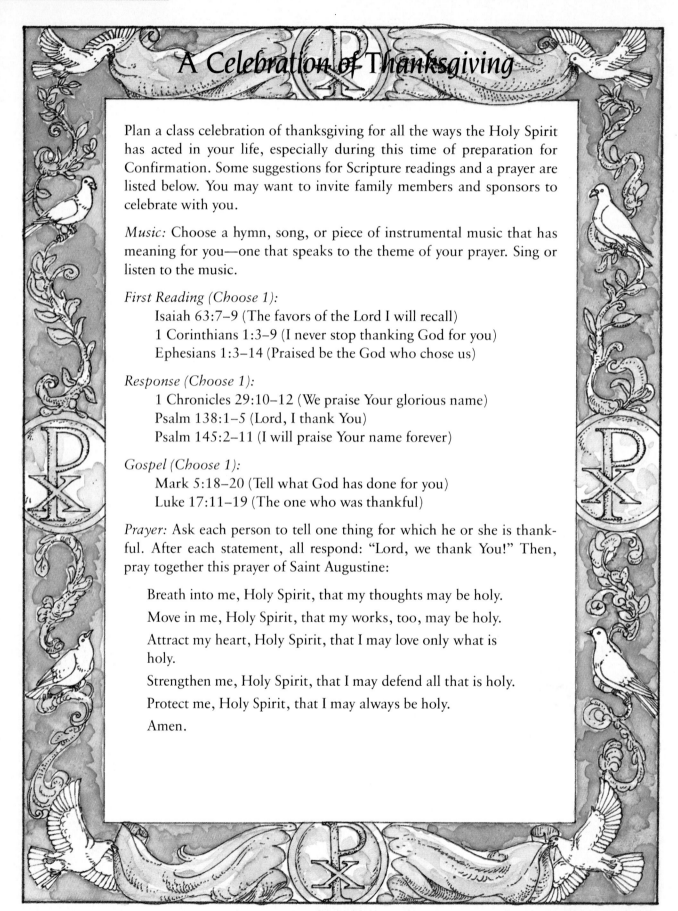

A Celebration of Thanksgiving

Plan a class celebration of thanksgiving for all the ways the Holy Spirit has acted in your life, especially during this time of preparation for Confirmation. Some suggestions for Scripture readings and a prayer are listed below. You may want to invite family members and sponsors to celebrate with you.

Music: Choose a hymn, song, or piece of instrumental music that has meaning for you—one that speaks to the theme of your prayer. Sing or listen to the music.

First Reading (Choose 1):
 Isaiah 63:7–9 (The favors of the Lord I will recall)
 1 Corinthians 1:3–9 (I never stop thanking God for you)
 Ephesians 1:3–14 (Praised be the God who chose us)

Response (Choose 1):
 1 Chronicles 29:10–12 (We praise Your glorious name)
 Psalm 138:1–5 (Lord, I thank You)
 Psalm 145:2–11 (I will praise Your name forever)

Gospel (Choose 1):
 Mark 5:18–20 (Tell what God has done for you)
 Luke 17:11–19 (The one who was thankful)

Prayer: Ask each person to tell one thing for which he or she is thankful. After each statement, all respond: "Lord, we thank You!" Then, pray together this prayer of Saint Augustine:

Breath into me, Holy Spirit, that my thoughts may be holy.

Move in me, Holy Spirit, that my works, too, may be holy.

Attract my heart, Holy Spirit, that I may love only what is holy.

Strengthen me, Holy Spirit, that I may defend all that is holy.

Protect me, Holy Spirit, that I may always be holy.

Amen.

Anointing   Signing with holy oil. Anointing is part of the sacraments of Baptism, Confirmation, and Holy Orders, and forms the central part of the sacrament of the Anointing of the Sick. Anointing symbolizes healing, strengthening, and consecrating.

Apathy   A word that means "lack of feeling." Apathy keeps people from acting in love and service, out of fear, helplessness, or indifference to the needs of others.

Baptism   The sacrament of initiation by which we become children of God and members of the Church.

Bishop   A word that means "overseer." Bishops are successors of the Apostles. Together with the pope, bishops make up the teaching and ruling authority of the Church. Each local Church community, or *diocese*, is headed by a bishop.

Blessed Sacrament   The name for Jesus Christ truly present in the Eucharist. In every Catholic church, the Blessed Sacrament—in the form of the Eucharistic Bread—is kept in the tabernacle. A lamp burns before the tabernacle at all times, to remind us of the presence of Jesus.

Canonization   The formal process by which the Church declares that a person has lived an outstanding Christian life and is worthy of being honored and imitated. One who has been canonized receives the title of "Saint"; his or her life is celebrated on a particular feast day.

Catholic Church   The most common name for our community of faith; the worldwide community of Christians who follow the pope and the bishops. Also called the *Roman Catholic Church*, because the traditional home diocese of the pope is Rome.

Chrism   Pure olive oil mixed with balsam (a fragrant spice) and blessed by the bishop. Chrism is used in the sacraments of Baptism, Confirmation, and Holy Orders. It differs from the unscented oils, also blessed by the bishop, that are used to anoint catechumens and the sick.

Common good   The principle of doing what is best for all involved.

Communion of saints   All members of the Church, living and dead, who are united in their common faith in Jesus.

Confession   The practice of telling one's sins to the priest which forms part of the sacrament of Reconciliation.

Confirmation   One of the seven sacraments of the Church. Confirmation celebrates the presence of the Holy Spirit in our lives; it *confirms*, or strengthens, our membership in the Church which began at Baptism.

Conscience   The inner power that helps us tell right from wrong. Every Catholic has the duty to "inform" his or her conscience through study of the Church's moral teachings and through prayer.

Conversion   Literally, "to turn around"; the process of bringing one's life into line with God's covenant of love.

Contemplation   Prayer and meditation that is focused on experiencing the presence of God.

Counsel   Another name for the gift of right judgment. This name reminds us that right judgment includes asking others for help, and offering good advice and example.

Courage   The gift of the Holy Spirit that helps us to act on our beliefs, to use our God-given talents bravely, and to reach out to others in loving service.

Covenant   A sacred, loving agreement or mutual relationship. God made a covenant with His People. Christian marriage is another example of covenant relationship.

Creed   From the Latin for "I believe"; a public statement of faith.

Deacon   A person ordained to serve the needs of the Christian community. Deacons may be "transitional" (in preparation for ordination to the priesthood) or "permanent." Permanent deacons may be married at the time of ordination; they are ordained to assist the bishop by preaching, teaching, serving the poor and the sick, and administering some sacraments. Most permanent deacons also hold regular jobs.

Diocese   A local Church community made up of a number of parishes, and overseen by a bishop. A diocese with a large Catholic population may be called an *archdiocese*, overseen by an archbishop or cardinal.

Encyclical letter   From the Greek words for a "message sent around"; an encyclical letter is a message sent by the pope to the bishops of the world, to be shared with all Catholics. A bishop or a group of bishops may publish a similar statement on Catholic teaching or social concerns, called a *pastoral letter*.

Eucharist   The sacrament which celebrates Jesus' saving action, and in which we share His Body and Blood. We celebrate this sacrament in the Mass. The word "Eucharist" means "thanksgiving."

Eucharistic prayer   The great prayer of thanksgiving in which we recall God's saving actions in history and the institution of the Eucharist at the Last Supper. The Eucharistic prayer or *canon* of the Mass also includes the consecration of the Eucharistic bread and wine, prayers for the blessing of the Holy Spirit, and prayers for all Catholics, living and dead. There are six major texts of the Eucharistic prayer approved for use in the United States, with several others approved specifically for Masses with children.

Faith   The virtue by which we put our trust in God and believe all that God has revealed—or made known—to us.

Fear of the Lord   A traditional name for the Holy Spirit's gift of wonder and awe. This name for the gift reminds us not to underestimate God's power and love.

Fortitude   Another name for the Holy Spirit's gift of courage. "Fortitude" means "the strength to endure."

Fruit of the Spirit   Qualities that indicate the presence of the Holy Spirit in one's life. Traditionally, these twelve qualities are: love (or charity), joy, peace, patience, kindness, generosity, faithfulness, gentleness (or modesty), self-control (or continency), goodness (or benignity), long-suffering (or longanimity), and chastity.

Gospels   The accounts of Jesus' life and teachings found in the New Testament of the Bible. There are four Gospels, named for their traditional authors: Saint Matthew, Saint Mark, Saint Luke, and Saint John. The word "gospel" means "good news."

Grace   A share in God's own life; friendship with God.

Heaven   Another name for the timeless or eternal kingdom of God; the state of perfect happiness with God.

Holiness   Likeness to Jesus Christ. The word "holy" means "whole" or "perfect." Each one of us is called to holiness.

Holy Communion   The reception of the Body and Blood of Jesus Christ in the Eucharist. The word "communion" means "oneness with"; in Holy Communion, we become one with Jesus and with other members of the Christian community.

Holy Spirit   The Third Person of the Trinity, who proceeds from the Father and the Son. We celebrate the presence of the Holy Spirit, who calls each of us to holiness, in the sacrament of Confirmation.

Identity   The sense of who we are and what we can do.

Immaculate Conception   A title of Mary that describes our belief that she was free from sin from the very beginning of her life. We celebrate the feast of the Immaculate Conception on December 8.

Integrity   The ability to act in accord with one's beliefs.

Intuition   An inner sense of how to act. Intuition is rooted in thought and reasoning, but it seems to move faster.

Jesus Christ   The name given to the Second Person of the Trinity, the Son of God. Jesus is both God and man. The name "Jesus" means "God saves His People"; the name "Christ" is Greek for Messiah or "anointed one."

Kingdom of God   The phrase Jesus used to describe God's powerful action in time and eternity. As Christians, we believe that the kingdom of God is both present "in our midst" as a promise, and yet to come as a state of perfect happiness, peace, and justice.

Knowledge   The gift of the Holy Spirit that helps us know—and be known by—God, ourselves, and others in a deeper way.

Liturgy   A public act of worship, including formal prayers and actions. The Mass is the highest form of liturgy.

Martyr   A person who dies for his or her beliefs. The word "martyr" is Greek for "witness." The earliest saints were martyrs who died during the Roman persecution of the Church.

Messiah   A Hebrew word that means "the anointed (or chosen) one," the Savior God promised to His People. We believe that Jesus is the Messiah.

Mission   A God-given task or duty in life. The mission of Jesus was to bring the Good News of God's saving love.

Missionary   A word meaning "one who is sent." Missionaries bring the Good News of Jesus to those who have not yet heard it.

Moral decisions   Choices that involve our Christian morality or sense of what is right (good for our relationship with God and others) and wrong (sinful).

Mystery   An article of faith (such as the existence of the Trinity, or the fact of Jesus' resurrection) that we believe, even though we do not fully understand it.

Nicene Creed   The profession of faith that we proclaim at Mass. The words of this prayer, which are based on the earlier Apostles' Creed, were developed at Church councils in Nicaea and Constantinople, around the 4th century A.D.

Obedience   The free submission of one's will to another. Obedience is a virtue, or positive spiritual quality, when we obey out of love, respect, and the desire to do what is right.

Parable   A special kind of teaching story that gives us an insight into the way God wants us to act. In His teaching, Jesus often used parables.

Paraclete   A scriptural term for the Holy Spirit; the word "paraclete" is Greek for "one who speaks for or defends the rights of others."

Parish   A community of Catholics, usually living in the same geographical area, who gather for Mass, the sacraments, and other activities at the same church. The spiritual leader of the parish is the pastor. A number of parishes make up a *diocese*.

Parousia   From the Greek word for "presence" or "arrival"; the end of the world as we know it, the Second Coming of Christ.

Pastor   From the Latin word for "shepherd"; the priest who is the spiritual leader of a parish. In areas where there are few priests, a pastoral administrator (a religious or layperson appointed by the bishop) serves as director of the parish activities.

Peer pressure   Pressure from people your age to go along with the crowd or to fit in. Peer pressure can be positive or negative, depending on whether the action you're being pressured into is right or wrong.

Pentecost   The Christian feast that celebrates the coming of the Holy Spirit to the Apostles. The Jews of Jesus' time celebrated a feast by the same name, commemorating the giving of the Ten Commandments to Moses. The word "Pentecost" means "fifty days"; the Spirit came to the Apostles fifty days after Jesus' resurrection.

Piety   Another name for the gift of reverence; a word that means "faithful obedience and love."

Pope   From the Latin word "Father"; the title of the leader of the Roman Catholic Church. The pope, as bishop of Rome, is the successor of Saint Peter.

Prayer   Talking to (and listening to) God. Prayer can take many forms—silent, spoken, or sung; formal or informal; individual or group. Traditionally, the four kinds of prayer are adoration, contrition, thanksgiving, and petition.

Priest   A person who has received the sacrament of Holy Orders and who serves the Church by celebrating the sacraments and by preaching. Diocesan priests are ordained to assist the bishop; religious priests are members of religious communities. In addition to parish work, priests work as teachers, hospital chaplains, counselors, and in many other areas of the Church's ministry.

Profession of faith   A public statement of faith. The Creed is our profession of faith.

Prophets   The wise men and women of the Old Testament who spoke for God and reminded people of the covenant.

Reconciliation   The sacrament in which Catholics confess their sins to a priest, express their sorrow, promise to do better, and receive absolution or sacramental forgiveness. The sacrament of Reconciliation is required in cases of mortal sin, and strongly encouraged at all times as a way to grow in faith.

Respect   The quality of honoring others, putting their needs before our own.

Resurrection   The rising of the body to be reunited with the immortal (undying) soul after death. We celebrate the resurrection of Jesus on Easter Sunday. His resurrection enables us to believe that God's power is greater than suffering and death, and that we, too, will share in eternal life.

Reverence   The gift of the Holy Spirit that moves us to show respect for God and for all the people and things God has made.

Right judgment   The gift of the Holy Spirit that helps us to make good decisions and act on our beliefs.

Rite   The formal words and actions that make up the liturgical celebration of a sacrament.

Sacraments of initiation   Baptism, Confirmation, and Eucharist are called sacraments of initiation (belonging) because they mark our membership in the Church. Early Christians celebrated these three sacraments together as one rite, a practice now renewed in the case of adults who wish to become Christians.

Sacrifice   An offering given to God, or something given up for the good of another. Jesus' suffering and death are the greatest sacrifice.

Self-esteem   The way we feel about who we are. People with high self-esteem feel good about themselves. They have a clear view of their own abilities.

Service   Action performed to meet the needs of others. The Greek word for service, "diakonia," is the root word of "deacon." The Latin word for service gives us the word "ministry." Christians are called to serve others.

Sin   From the Hebrew for "missing the mark"; the deliberate choice to turn away from God's love, expressed in wrong action or in failure to act the right way.

Son of God   A title of Jesus, applied to Him in Scripture by Saint Peter, Martha, and others who recognized that He was the Messiah.

Talent   A special gift, skill, or ability. Each of us has been given talents by God, to develop and to use for others. This word comes from the Parable of the Talents (Coins) in Scripture.

Theology   A word that means "the study of God." Theologians devote their lives to learning about God and about our faith. Guided by the teaching authority of the pope and the bishops, theology helps us to know God.

Tradition   The beliefs passed along from generation to generation by the Church. All Church teaching is based on God's revelation (making Himself known) in Scripture and tradition.

Trinity   The mystery of three Divine Persons—Father, Son, and Holy Spirit—in one God.

Understanding   The gift of the Holy Spirit that helps us see the truth in our relationship with God, with others, and with ourselves.

Vice   A bad habit or way of acting. Growing in faith means avoiding vices.

Virtue   A good habit or way of acting. Growing in faith means practicing virtues.

Vocation   A word that literally means "calling"; the call from God to live out our Christian commitment—to grow in holiness and to serve others—in a particular way. Marriage, priesthood, religious life, and the single life are all examples of vocation.

Wisdom   The gift of the Holy Spirit that helps us see God, ourselves, and others clearly—as God sees us.

Witness   To give testimony to one's beliefs by public action or proclamation. Christians are called to give witness to the Good News of Jesus Christ.

Wonder and awe   The gift of the Holy Spirit that helps us remain open to the surprising, delightful, loving presence of God in our lives, and to respond with goodness and love.

Worship   The act of showing reverence and honor to God.

Prayers

The Sign of the Cross

In the name of the Father,
and of the Son,
and of the Holy Spirit.
Amen.

The Lord's Prayer

Our Father, who art in heaven,
hallowed be Thy name.
Thy kingdom come; Thy will be done
on earth as it is in heaven.
Give us this day our daily bread,
and forgive us our trespasses
as we forgive those who trespass against us;
and lead us not into temptation,
but deliver us from evil.
Amen.

The Hail Mary

Hail, Mary, full of grace,
the Lord is with thee.
Blessed art thou among women,
and blessed is the Fruit of thy womb, Jesus.
Holy Mary, Mother of God,
pray for us sinners, now,
and at the hour of our death.
Amen.

Glory to the Father

Glory to the Father,
and to the Son,
and to the Holy Spirit,
as it was in the beginning,
is now, and will be forever.
Amen.

The Apostles' Creed

I believe in God, the Father almighty,
Creator of heaven and earth.
I believe in Jesus Christ,
His only Son, our Lord.
He was conceived
by the power of the Holy Spirit,
and born of the Virgin Mary.
He suffered under Pontius Pilate,
was crucified, died, and was buried.
He descended to the dead.
On the third day He rose again.
He ascended into heaven,
and is seated at the right hand of the Father.
He will come again
to judge the living and the dead.
I believe in the Holy Spirit,
the holy catholic Church,
the communion of saints,
the forgiveness of sins,
the resurrection of the body,
and the life everlasting.
Amen.

Prayer to the Holy Spirit

Come, Holy Spirit,
fill the hearts of Your faithful.
And kindle in them the fire of Your love.
Send forth Your Spirit
and they shall be created.
And You will renew the face of the earth.
  Lord, by the light of the Holy Spirit
  You have taught the hearts of Your
  faithful.
  In the same Spirit,
  help us to relish what is right
  and always rejoice in Your consolation.
  We ask this through Christ our Lord.
Amen.

Memorare

Remember, most loving Virgin Mary,
never was it heard
that anyone who turned to you for help
was left unaided.
Inspired by this confidence,
though burdened by my sins,
I run to your protection,
for you are my Mother.
Mother of the Word of God,
do not despise my words of pleading
but be merciful and hear my prayer.
Amen.

Salve, Regina

Hail, Holy Queen, Mother of mercy,
hail, our life, our sweetness, and our hope.
To you we cry, the children of Eve;
to you we send up our sighs,
mourning and weeping in this land of exile.
Turn, then, most gracious advocate,
your eyes of mercy toward us;
lead us home at last and show us
the blessed Fruit of your womb, Jesus.
O clement, O loving, O sweet Virgin Mary,
pray for us who turn to you for hope.

Prayer of Faith, Hope, and Love

My God, I believe in You,
I trust in You,
I love You above all things,
with all my heart and mind and strength.
I love You because You are supremely good
and worth loving;
and because I love You,
I am sorry with all my heart for having
offended You.
Lord, have mercy on me, a sinner.
Amen.

Act of Contrition

My God,
I am sorry for my sins with all my heart.
In choosing to do wrong
and failing to do good,
I have sinned against You
whom I should love above all things.
I firmly intend, with Your help,
to do penance,
to sin no more,
and to avoid whatever leads me to sin.
Our Savior Jesus Christ
suffered and died for us.
In His name, my God, have mercy.

Morning Prayer

Almighty God,
You have given us this day:
strengthen us with Your power
and keep us from falling into sin,
so that whatever we say or think or do
may be in Your service
and for the sake of Your kingdom.
We ask this through Christ our Lord.
Amen.

Evening Prayer

Lord, watch over us this night.
By Your strength, may we rise at daybreak
to rejoice in the resurrection
of Christ, Your Son,
who lives and reigns for ever and ever.
Amen.

Important Things to Remember

The Ten Commandments

1. I, the Lord, am your God. You shall not have other gods besides Me.
2. You shall not take the name of the Lord, your God, in vain.
3. Remember to keep holy the sabbath day.
4. Honor your father and your mother.
5. You shall not kill.
6. You shall not commit adultery.
7. You shall not steal.
8. You shall not bear false witness against your neighbor.
9. You shall not covet your neighbor's wife.
10. You shall not covet anything that belongs to your neighbor.

—based on Exodus 20:2–17

The Beatitudes

Blessed are the poor in spirit, for theirs is the kingdom of heaven.

Blessed are they who mourn, for they will be comforted.

Blessed are the meek, for they will inherit the land.

Blessed are they who hunger and thirst for righteousness, for they will be satisfied.

Blessed are the merciful, for they will be shown mercy.

Blessed are the clean of heart, for they will see God.

Blessed are the peacemakers, for they will be called children of God.

Blessed are they who are persecuted for the sake of righteousness, for theirs is the kingdom of heaven.

—based on Matthew 5:3–10

The Rules of the Church

1. Take part in the Eucharist every Sunday and holy day. Do no unnecessary work on Sunday.
2. Receive the sacraments frequently.
3. Study the Good News of Jesus Christ.
4. Follow the marriage laws of the Church.
5. Support the People of God.
6. Do penance on certain days.
7. Support the missionary efforts of the Church.

The Corporal Works of Mercy

Feed the hungry.
Give drink to the thirsty.
Clothe the naked.
Shelter the homeless.
Visit the sick.
Visit the imprisoned.
Bury the dead.

The Spiritual Works of Mercy

Help the sinner.
Teach the ignorant.
Counsel the doubtful.
Comfort the sorrowful.
Bear wrongs patiently.
Forgive injuries.
Pray for the living and the dead.

The Mysteries of the Rosary

Joyful Mysteries

1. The Annunciation (Mary agrees to be the Mother of God)
2. The Visitation (Mary visits her cousin Elizabeth)
3. The Nativity (Jesus is born in Bethlehem)
4. The Presentation (Mary and Joseph take Jesus to the Temple for the first time)

5. The Finding in the Temple (After the young Jesus has been lost, Mary and Joseph find Him teaching in the Temple)

Sorrowful Mysteries
1. The Agony in the Garden (Jesus prays before His arrest)
2. The Scourging (Jesus is beaten)
3. The Crowning with Thorns (Jesus is mocked)
4. The Way of the Cross (Jesus carries His cross to Calvary)
5. The Crucifixion (Jesus dies for us)

Glorious Mysteries
1. The Resurrection (Jesus rises from the dead)
2. The Ascension (Jesus returns to His Father)
3. Pentecost (The Holy Spirit comes to the Apostles)
4. The Assumption (Mary is taken, body and soul, to heaven)
5. The Coronation (Mary is crowned the Queen of Heaven and Earth)

The Way of the Cross
1. Jesus is condemned to death.
2. Jesus takes up His cross.
3. Jesus falls the first time.
4. Jesus meets His sorrowful Mother.
5. Simon of Cyrene helps to carry the cross.
6. Veronica wipes the face of Jesus.
7. Jesus falls a second time.
8. The women of Jerusalem weep for Jesus.
9. Jesus falls the third time.
10. Jesus is stripped of His garments.
11. Jesus is nailed to the cross.
12. Jesus dies on the cross.
13. Jesus is laid in the arms of His Mother.

14. Jesus is laid in the tomb.
15. *[Sometimes added]* Jesus rises from the dead.

The Seven Sacraments
Sacraments of Initiation
    Baptism
    Confirmation
    Eucharist

Sacraments of Healing
    Reconciliation
    Anointing of the Sick

Sacraments of Vocation
    Marriage
    Holy Orders

Holy Days and Special Feasts in the United States
The Solemnity of Mary, Mother of God (January 1)
Ash Wednesday (the Wednesday before the First Sunday of Lent)
Palm Sunday (The Sunday before Easter)
Holy Thursday (the Thursday in Holy Week)
Good Friday (the Friday in Holy Week)
Holy Saturday (the day before Easter)
The Resurrection of Our Lord/Easter Sunday (date changes)
Ascension Thursday (40 days after Easter)
Pentecost (50 days after Easter)
The Assumption of Mary (August 15)
All Saints' Day (November 1)
All Souls' Day (November 2)
The Immaculate Conception of Mary (December 8)
Our Lady of Guadalupe, Patron of the Americas (December 12)
The Nativity of Our Lord/Christmas (December 25)

The Order of the Mass

Introductory Rites

- *The Entrance Procession* The priest, deacon, and ministers enter the church.
- *The Greeting* The priest greets the community in the name of the Father, and of the Son, and of the Holy Spirit.
- *The Penitential Rite* We pray for God's mercy and forgiveness.
- *Glory to God* We sing or pray the ancient hymn in honor of God's goodness.
- *The Opening Prayer* The priest prays to God in our name.

The Liturgy of the Word

- *The First Reading* A reading from the Old Testament, the Hebrew Scriptures.
- *Psalm Response* We sing or pray a psalm together.
- *The Second Reading* From the letters of Saint Paul or another part of the New Testament.
- *Alleluia* We sing or pray a verse in honor of Jesus, with the Hebrew response that means "Praise the Lord!"
- *The Gospel* The priest or deacon proclaims a passage from one of the four Gospels.
- *The Homily* The priest or deacon helps us "break open" and understand God's Word.
- *The Creed* We stand to proclaim our beliefs.
- *The Prayer of the Faithful* We ask God to remember the needs of His People everywhere.

The Liturgy of the Eucharist

- *The Preparation of the Gifts* The gifts of bread and wine are brought to the altar, along with our contributions to the support of the parish.
- *The Offering* The priest prepares the gifts and prays a blessing prayer.
- *The Preface* The priest prays the introduction to the Eucharistic prayer. We respond, "Holy, Holy, Holy Lord. . ."
- *The Eucharistic Prayer* In this prayer of thanksgiving, the priest uses the words of Jesus to consecrate the bread and wine. We proclaim our faith in Jesus. The prayer recalls God's saving actions and remembers all believers, living and dead. The Eucharistic prayer concludes with a doxology, or praise of the Trinity, to which we respond with the Great Amen.
- *The Lord's Prayer* We pray together in the words Jesus taught us.
- *The Sign of Peace* We offer one another a sign of Christ's peace.
- *The Breaking of the Bread* The priest breaks the Host and mixes part of it with the Eucharistic Wine. We pray, "Lamb of God . . ."
- *The Communion* We receive the Body and Blood of Christ. We sing or pray in thanksgiving.

Concluding Rites

- *The Closing Prayer* The priest prays to God in our name.
- *The Blessing* The priest blesses us in the name of the Father, and of the Son, and of the Holy Spirit.
- *The Dismissal* We are sent forth to love and serve the Lord.

How to Go to Confession

Before Receiving the Sacrament

- Examine your conscience quietly.
- Say a prayer to the Holy Spirit. Ask the Holy Spirit to be with you and to help you make a good confession.
- Wait quietly for your turn to enter the Reconciliation room or confessional. Be courteous to others who are waiting.

Steps in the Sacrament of Reconciliation [Individual Penitent]

- The priest greets you in the name of the Father, and of the Son, and of the Holy Spirit.
- The priest says a prayer to help you trust in God. You answer, "Amen."
- The priest may read (or may ask you to read) a passage from Scripture to remind you of God's love and forgiveness.
- You tell your sins to the priest. Then, he talks with you about how you might make better choices.
- The priest gives you a penance.
- The priest invites you to express your sorrow to God. Then, you pray an Act of Contrition.
- The priest extends his hands over your head and prays the prayer of absolution. You answer, "Amen."
- The priest prays, "Give thanks to the Lord, for He is good." You answer, "His mercy endures forever."
- The priest says, "The Lord has freed you from your sins. Go in peace."

[With a Group]

- The Reconciliation service may begin with a hymn.
- The priest greets the penitents.
- The priest prays the Opening Prayer. All respond, "Amen."
- One or more readings from Scripture are proclaimed, with a psalm response if desired. If there is only one reading, it should be from the Gospels.
- The priest or deacon preaches a brief homily.
- There is time for an Examination of Conscience, which may be silent reflection or a litany-type prayer.
- All pray together an Act of Contrition or Litany of Sorrow, followed by the Lord's Prayer.
- Confession and absolution are carried out individually at this time. In situations where there are too few priests, and the opportunity for individual confession will not occur for more than a month, general absolution may be given. Penitents who have received general absolution must still make an individual confession at the first opportunity.
- The congregation gathers to sing a song or pray in praise of God's mercy.
- The priests prays the Concluding Prayer. All respond, "Amen."
- The priests blesses those present in the name of the Father, and of the Son, and of the Holy Spirit.
- The priest or deacon dismisses the assembly by saying. "The Lord has freed you from your sins. Go in peace." All respond, "Thanks be to God."

After Receiving the Sacrament

- Spend a few moments in quiet thanksgiving. If you have been given prayers to say as your penance, you may do so now. If the priest has asked you to carry out some penitential action, plan how you will do this.
- Do not talk with others about your confession. Do not ask others about their confession.

Participating in the Sacraments

Eucharist

- To receive Communion worthily, you must be free from mortal sin and have expressed sorrow for any venial sin committed since your last confession.
- In honor of Jesus, Catholics fast from all food and drink (except water or medicine) for one hour before receiving Holy Communion.
- You can receive the Host in your hand or on your tongue. When the priest or Eucharistic minister says, "The Body of Christ," you answer, "Amen."
- At certain times, you may also receive Communion from the Cup. The priest or Eucharistic minister will say, "The Blood of Christ." You answer, "Amen." The priest or Eucharistic minister will offer the Cup to you; take a small sip.
- Catholics are required to receive Communion at least once a year, during the Easter season, but you should receive Communion as frequently as you can, to strengthen your relationship with Jesus with the Christian community. As long as you are in the state of grace (free from mortal sin), you may receive Communion once a day.

Reconciliation

- Sin is a deliberate choice to turn against God or to break God's Law. Mortal sin is serious or grave; it separates us from God's grace. Venial sin is less serious, but still damaging.
- In order to commit mortal sin, the action must be seriously wrong. You must know that the action is seriously wrong. And you must choose—on your own, without threats or pressure—to do it anyway. No one can commit mortal sin by accident.

- To receive forgiveness for mortal sin, you must confess your sin to a priest; be sincerely sorry for the sin and willing to make up for the wrong you have done; agree to do penance; receive absolution from the priest.
- Participation in the sacrament of Reconciliation is required once a year for all Catholics who have committed mortal sin. But since mortal sin keeps you from receiving Communion, it is important to confess mortal sin as soon as possible.
- Reconciliation is also important—though not required—in the case of venial sin. Frequent, regular confession of venial sin will help you overcome bad habits and learn to follow Jesus more closely.
- You may confess to the priest in a Reconciliation room (either face-to-face or separated by a screen) or in a confessional. In either case, it is your choice whether or not to identify yourself to the priest. The priest is bound by a sacred promise not to tell anyone else what he hears during sacramental confession.